Global Perspectives

Reading & Writing   Book 2

by

Noriko Nakanishi

Nicholas Musty

Shoko Otake

Tam Shuet Ying

Mary Ellis

photographs by

© iStockphoto

音声ファイルのダウンロード／ストリーミング

CD マーク表示がある箇所は、音声を弊社 HP より無料でダウンロード／ストリーミングすることができます。下記 URL の書籍詳細ページに音声ダウンロードアイコンがございますのでそちらから自習用音声としてご活用ください。

https://www.seibido.co.jp/ad689

Global Perspectives
Reading & Writing Book 2

はしがき

　インターネットの発達により、日本国内にいても、英文を読み、自分が伝えたいことを発信することができる時代になりました。また、自分で英文を読んだり書いたりしなくても、大まかな内容ならば日本語に翻訳されたものを読み、日本語で書いた文を英語に自動翻訳する技術はすでに一般的になっています。しかし、単に概要を把握したり伝えたりするだけでなく、相手の真意を読み取り、分かりやすく伝えるためには、文のニュアンスを読み取って論点を整理し、相手の文化や考え方の背景を尊重しながら自分の考えを自分の言葉で順序よく伝える必要があります。

　さらに、同じ内容を伝えようとする英文であっても、Eメール文、ブログ、チャット、張り紙、パンフレットのように日常的に目にする英文にはそれぞれ特徴的な書き方がありますし、学術的なエッセイや論文には、決まったスタイルがあります。一方、英文を機械翻訳で和訳したものを読み、日本語で作文したものを機械翻訳で英訳していると、途中どこかのプロセスで誤訳や場面にふさわしくない表現が紛れ込む危険性がつきまといます。場面や状況に応じて文章を効率よく読み、書き分けるコミュニケーション力が、今後の社会では一層求められます。

　本書のねらいは、学習者が大学入学までに培ってきた以下の「三つの柱（文部科学省、2018年3月公示）」を引き継ぎ、さらに発展させることです。

　（1）何を理解しているか、何ができるか（知識・技能）

　（2）理解していること・できることをどう使うか（思考力・判断力・表現力）

　（3）どのように社会・世界と関わり、よりよい人生を送るか（学びに向かう力・人間性）

　本書の Book 1 では大学生が日常的に経験する「大学生活」「心と体の健康」のようなトピック、Book 2 では「学術研究」「科学とは」のような、大学生にふさわしい学際的なトピックを扱います。ユニットごとのトピックに関連するパッセージを読んでリーディング力を養うだけでなく、情報を整理し、多様な角度から検討した上で、論理的・客観的に自分の意見を述べるための批判的思考力をつけることを目的としています。近年の社会情勢を反映させた話題や、賛否が分かれることがらを取り上げたパッセージを読んだうえで、自分の意見を整理して英語で述べるためのライティングアウトラインの作成へとつなげます。本書を通して、学習者が英語のリーディング力やライティング力を伸ばすだけでなく、思考力・判断力・表現力や積極性・人間性を養うきっかけとなることを願っています。

　最後に、本書の出版にあたり、趣旨をご理解くださり、きめ細やかなアドバイスでサポートくださった（株）成美堂編集部の中澤ひろ子氏に、心から感謝を申し上げます。

2023 年 11 月

筆者一同

本書の構成 / 使い方

❶ Warm-up

各ユニットに関連したトピックについて4つの選択肢の中から自分の知識や考えに近いものを選び、ウォーミングアップをしましょう。時間に余裕があれば、なぜその選択肢を選んだか説明し、クラスメイトと意見交換しましょう。

❷ Words in Focus

各ユニットに関連した用語を予め確認しましょう。単に英単語を和訳するのではなく、用語をネット検索して、トピックと関連する背景知識を身につけておきましょう。

❸ Casual Reading

ホームページやメール、ブログ、チャット、張り紙、パンフレットような日常的に目にする短いパッセージを読みましょう。パッセージ内の3か所は穴埋め問題になっています。前後の文脈を読み取ってふさわしい語句を選択しましょう。続いて、内容確認問題が3問あります。そのうちの1つは、パッセージに加えて、スマホ画面やシンボル、広告、図表のような情報も参考にして回答する問題です。TOEIC Part 7 ダブルパッセージ問題の練習としても活用することができます。

❹ Reading Tips

上記の短いパッセージの要点をまとめた穴埋め問題に回答し、パッセージを読む際のコツをつかみましょう。以下は、各ユニットで紹介されるリーディングのコツです。

Unit	コツ	Unit	コツ
1	Main idea and details (1)	7	Sequencing
2	Dealing with unknown words	8	Comparison and contrast
3	Cause and effect	9	Main idea and details (2)
4	Understanding timelines	10	Inference (1)
5	Similarities and differences	11	Inference (2)
6	Categorizing	12	Paraphrasing

❺ Academic Reading

　Book 1 は 280〜400 語前後、Book 2 では 320〜470 語前後のまとまったパッセージを読みましょう。パッセージの長さは、Unit 1 から 12 にかけて少しずつ長くなるよう調整されています。初めて読む際には、時間を測りながら全体の内容を把握する練習をしてください。ページの下には、wpm（words per minute、1分間当たりに読める単語数）を計算するための式が表示されています。ある程度の内容を理解しながら読むことができる速さの記録をとりましょう。隣のページには、パッセージ中、太字で示されているキーワードの意味を確認する問題や、内容を確認する問題があります。内容確認問題は、基本的に1パラグラフにつき1題ずつ出題されています。読んだ内容を把握できているか確認しましょう。

❻ Writing Tips

　上記のパッセージのパラグラフ構成を理解するための穴埋め問題に回答し、英文ライティングのコツをつかみましょう。以下は、各ユニットで紹介されるライティングのコツです。

Unit	コツ	Unit	コツ
1	What is a paragraph?	7	Narrative essay
2	APA (1) Making a references page	8	Persuasive essay
3	Formal vs. informal writing	9	APA (2) In-text citations
4	Different types of transitions	10	What is a good thesis statement?
5	Descriptive essay	11	Self-reflective writing
6	Written vs. spoken English	12	APA (3) When you paraphrase/don't paraphrase

❼ Writing Outline

　各ユニットに関連したトピックについて、自分の考えを書くためのアウトラインをまとめましょう。アウトラインは、基本的に「Introduction（導入）」と「Conclusion（結論）」の間に「Body（本論）」を挟み込む構成になっています。Writing Tips で学んだライティングのコツも参考にしながら、書きたい内容の枠組みを決めましょう。

CONTENTS

EnglishCentralのご案内

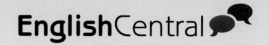

　本テキスト各ユニットの「Academic Reading」で学習する音声は、オンライン学習システム「EnglishCentral」で学習することができます。

　EnglishCentralでは動画の視聴や単語のディクテーションのほか、動画のセリフを音読し録音すると、コンピュータが発音を判定します。PCのwebだけでなく、スマートフォン、タブレットではアプリでも学習できます。リスニング、スピーキング、語彙力向上のため、ぜひ活用してください。

　EnglishCentralの利用にはアカウントとアクセスコードの登録が必要です。登録方法については下記ページにアクセスしてください。
（画像はすべてサンプルで、実際の教材とは異なります）

https://www.seibido.co.jp/englishcentral/pdf/ectextregister.pdf

見る

本文内でわからなかった単語は1クリックでその場で意味を確認

スロー再生　　　日英字幕（ON/OFF可）

学ぶ

音声を聴いて空欄の単語をタイピング。ゲーム感覚で楽しく単語を覚える

話す

動画のセリフを音読し録音、コンピュータが発音を判定。

日本人向けに専門開発された音声認識によってスピーキング力を%で判定

ネイティブと自分が録音した発音を聞き比べ練習に生かすことができます

苦手な発音記号を的確に判断し、単語を緑、黄、赤の3色で表示

Academic Research

学術的な研究について考えよう

Warm-up: *Share your ideas.*

Which of the following is most difficult for you when learning English?

a. Vocabulary.

b. Grammar.

c. Pronunciation.

d. Spelling.

> *I chose answer _____ , because .....*
> ....
> ....
> ....

Words in Focus: *Search the internet for words and phrases.* 1-02

❑ APA

❑ couch

❑ error

❑ humanities

❑ in-text citation

❑ literature

❑ MLA

❑ publication

❑ social science

❑ spell-checker

The Global Times May 25

Are spell-checkers foolproof? The case of funny spelling mistakes

When you write in English, there are many things you need to be careful about. However, some people don't worry about spelling. They say it is because spell-checkers can correct errors for them. But is that really true?

First of all, let's look at a type of spelling error which involves just one letter. For example, in one class, a student was writing an essay for the topic "The person I admire the most." He wanted to explain how much he admired his "coach," but he wrote " 1 " instead. We must say that the "couch" is a nice piece of furniture, but not a person to be admired. However, the spell-checker didn't catch this mistake, because both "coach" and "couch" are real words.

Let's look at another example. This is the type of spelling error that sounds the same as the intended word. The sign below says "No Smoking Aloud." Of course, nobody can smoke 2 , because it is very difficult to speak while smoking at the same time. People who made the sign must have wanted to say, "No Smoking Allowed!" Again, spell-checkers cannot catch this type of error because both "aloud" and "allowed" are existing English words.

Finally, if spell-checkers can fail, what should we do? The solution is straightforward: use a 3 when you write. It can be a web-based or paper dictionary, but it would help you increase your vocabulary and spot the errors we discussed here.

1. Choose the best answer to complete the missing words in the passage.

1.	2.	3.
(A) coach	(A) aloud	(A) computer
(B) couch	(B) loudly	(B) dictionary
(C) poach	(C) louder	(C) paper
(D) touch	(D) loudest	(D) spell-checker

2. Read the passage and choose the best answer to each question.

   1. Why don't some people pay attention to spelling?

   (A) Because they write about many things.

   (B) Because they worry about other things when they write.

   (C) Because they have few chances to write in English.

   (D) Because spell-checkers can correct mistakes.

   2. Why did the student write "couch" instead of "coach"?

   (A) The pronunciation of the two words is the same.

   (B) The meaning of the two words is similar.

   (C) They both have similar letters.

   (D) They both have the same meaning.

   3. Look at the sign. Which of the following is true?

   (A) It is fine to smoke here.

   (B) Smoking is harmful to your health.

   (C) Video recording is prohibited here.

   (D) The sign has a spelling error.

Reading Tips: *Main idea and details (1)*

読者にとって読みやすい英文の多くは、1つずつの段落（paragraph）内で議論する内容がはっきりと topic sentence として示され、それを説明するための詳細が述べられています。前ページの4つの段落それぞれの topic sentence を以下に書き出しましょう。

Paragraph	Topic sentence
1	They say it is because _____ - _____ _____ _____ _____ _____ _____ . But _____ _____ _____ _____?
2	First of all, let's look at _____ _____ _____ _____ _____ _____ _____ _____ ____ _____ .
3	Let's _____ _____ _____ _____ .
4	Finally, if _____ - _____ _____ _____ , _____ _____ _____ ____?

Comparing APA and MLA

Have you heard of "APA" and "MLA"? They are different styles of **citing** information. When you **cite** something in a paper, it shows the origin of your information. This allows you to support the ideas presented in your paper. APA and MLA are two different ways of doing the same thing. This essay will discuss their similarities and differences.

5

First, let us look at the specific similarities of the two styles. For both styles, you have two steps to **cite** information. In the first step, you need to add an in-text citation next to the sentence (or after the paragraph) where you used an idea from a **source**. In the second step, you add a list of all **references** at the end of your paper. Both APA and MLA styles need to

10 include an author, publication year, and title.

Second, what are the significant differences between the two styles? APA stands for "American Psychological Association." This style is used often in **psychology**, education, and the social sciences. Conversely, MLA stands for "Modern Language Association." It's also a

15 style of **citing** information, but is used for the **humanities**, such as literature, cultural studies, and history.

Third, let us look at the finer differences between the two styles. For example, when doing in-text citations, you need the publication year for APA style. This is because in

20 scientific writing, talking about recent publications is very important, as well as knowing which year a certain idea originated from. On the other hand, in MLA in-text citations, including the page number is important because it's often used to **cite** ideas in literature. In APA style citations, page numbers are used only if you include a direct quote in your paper.

25 In conclusion, APA and MLA are different ways to **cite** information. What is important is that whatever style you choose, you must follow their rules to correctly show the direct **source** of your information.

Table 1. In-text citations and list of references in APA and MLA styles.

Style	In-text citations	List of references
APA	(Bennett, 2009, p.45)	Bennett, K. (2009). English academic style manuals: A survey. *Journal of English for Academic Purposes, 8*(1), 43–54.
MLA	(Bennett 45)	Bennett, Karen. "English Academic Style Manuals: A Survey." *Journal of English for Academic Purposes*, vol. 8, no. 1, 2009, pp. 43–54.

Your Reading Speed: **323** words ÷ _____ seconds × 60 = _____ wpm

1. Choose the phrase that is related to each word / phrase.

1. cite ( )
2. source ( )
3. reference ( )
4. psychology ( )
5. humanities ( )

(a) description of works mentioned in a paper
(b) the study of human culture
(c) the study of the human mind
(d) to refer to someone's ideas
(e) where you got your information from

2. Read the passage and choose the best answer to each question.

1. What are APA and MLA?
   (A) The names of newspaper companies.
   (B) Locations where academic conferences are held.
   (C) Techniques for delivering oral presentations.
   (D) Styles for indicating the source of your information.

2. Which one is NOT mentioned as a similarity between APA and MLA styles?
   (A) They both require two steps.
   (B) They both show how long a paper is.
   (C) They both require a list of the sources.
   (D) They both show how to cite information.

3. In what field would a student be likely to write a paper in MLA style?
   (A) Education.
   (B) Literature.
   (C) Psychology.
   (D) Social sciences.

4. Which is more likely to apply to a student studying literature?
   (A) The publication year is necessary.
   (B) Recent publications are preferred.
   (C) Scientific logic is important.
   (D) The page number is always required.

5. What is the author's conclusion about APA and MLA?
   (A) APA is better than MLA.
   (B) You should use both styles.
   (C) MLA is better than APA.
   (D) You should follow their rules.

A paragraph is a series of sentences that are related to a single topic. The passage on page 4 has five paragraphs. For the fourth paragraph of this passage, separate each sentence according to the structure below. Can you see how each paragraph is structured so the writer can easily compare/contrast APA and MLA?

Topic sentence	Third, let us look at the _____ _____ _____ _____ _____ _____.
Body (APA)	For example, when _____ _____-_____ _____, _____ _____ _____ _____ _____ for APA style.
Body (MLA)	_____ _____ _____ _____, in MLA in-text citations, _____ _____ _____ _____ is important because it's often used to _____ _____ _____ _____.

There are many different types of source for academic research besides web pages. Choose one source from (A) books, (B) academic journals, (C) official databases, or (D) mass media, and describe it in detail.

Introduction	I recommend using [source type] for academic research. This means [what]. It is [why]. Students should [how].
Detail 1: "What"	To explain in detail, [source type] is....
Detail 2: "Why"	The reason that I recommend using [source type] is....
Detail 3: "How"	Students who use [source type] should remember to....
Summary	As you can see, [source type] is useful for academic research because [why]. Be sure to [how].

Social Issues in Japan

日本の社会について考えよう

Warm-up: *Share your ideas.*

Which of the following issues in Japan are you most concerned about?

- **a.** Aging population.
- **b.** Gender inequality.
- **c.** Mental health issues.
- **d.** Discrimination against minority groups.

I chose answer _____ , because .....
....
....
....

Words in Focus: *Search the internet for words and phrases.* 1-06

- ❑ deduction
- ❑ hometown tax program
- ❑ labor force
- ❑ objective
- ❑ population imbalance

- ❑ proficiency
- ❑ recruit
- ❑ revenue
- ❑ teleworking
- ❑ universal design

1-07

Universal Design App Project Meeting

Objective: Provide easy-to-use apps for everyone

Date: May 7th Time: 9:30–11:00	Location: Room D302 Attendees: Project team members

1. Completed Project Review

STAGE 1: Provide easy-to-use apps for <u>all generations.</u>

STAGE 2: Provide easy-to-use apps for <u>all people with/without special needs.</u>

2. Ongoing Project Overview

STAGE 3: Provide easy-to-use apps for <u>all people with different language proficiencies.</u>

3. Project Teams

The project will be launched by two teams, Multilingual and Graphics.

✔ Multilingual team is responsible for ⬚ 1 ⬚ (Japanese, English, Chinese).

✔ ⬚ 2 ⬚ team is responsible for designing icons.

These teams work together when necessary.

Each team is divided into five sections. The section leaders are:

	Promotion	Manual	App displays	Payment procedure	Customer support
Multilingual	Ken	James	Lily	Dave	Asha
Graphics	Sofia	Anna	Eric	Mari	Lucas

4. Schedule

To be completed in the next seven days:

✔ **Promotion:** Determine target customers.

✔ **Manual:** Make a list of manuals for our apps that are already on the market.

✔ **App displays:** Make a list of all the app displays that are already on the market.

✔ **Payment procedure:** Check in which language our current customers read credit card payment instructions.

✔ ⬚ 3 ⬚ : Recruit additional staff to respond to customer inquiries.

5. Next Meeting

May 14th, 9:30–11:00 in Room D302

1. **Choose the best answer to complete the missing words in the passage.**

1. (A) transfer
   (B) transition
   (C) translation
   (D) transport

2. (A) Customer
   (B) Graphics
   (C) Manual
   (D) Promotion

3. (A) Customer support
   (B) Credit card
   (C) Insurance
   (D) Design

2. **Read the passage and choose the best answer to each question.**

1. What is the goal of this project?
   (A) To improve the university system.
   (B) To create an easy-to-use app.
   (C) To do physical exercise.
   (D) To learn a foreign language.

2. Look at the smartphone screen. In what stage was this app developed?
   (A) Stage 1.
   (B) Stage 2.
   (C) Stage 3.
   (D) None of the above.

3. What is James likely to do in the next seven days?
   (A) Determine target customers.
   (B) Find manuals for their current apps.
   (C) Collect displays of their current apps.
   (D) Check card payment methods.

Reading Tips: *Dealing with unknown words*

英文を読んでいて知らない単語に出くわした時、前後の文から意味を推測しながら読み進めていく習慣をつけると、英語を英語で考え素早く読み進めることにつながります。前ページのタイトルで示されている "universal design" に関する文を書き出し、その意味を推測してみましょう。

Universal design とは？（文脈）	（推測）
STAGE 1: Provide easy-to-use apps for _____ _____.	すべての世代に向けたデザイン。
STAGE 2: Provide easy-to-use apps for _____ _____ _____ / _____ _____ _____.	特別な支援の必要性を問わないデザイン。
STAGE 3: Provide easy-to-use apps for _____ _____ _____ _____ _____.	様々な言語力に対応したデザイン。

Measures to increase tax revenue in depopulated areas

Young people tend to go to large cities to study and work. They usually pay taxes to the local government where they live, not where they were born. Thus, the local government with a smaller working population receives less tax revenue. Insufficient tax revenue leads to insufficient public services, making even more people try to leave the area. The population
5 imbalance eventually results in a **vicious cycle**. In this essay, three ways to address the population **disparity** problem will be discussed.

One way is to keep the working population in remote places. In recent years, more and more companies have been allowing employees to work outside their offices. If workers are
10 allowed to work from home, they will no longer have to move to cities. With teleworking, work can be "achieved with the help of ICTs and conducted outside the employer's locations" (International Labour Organization, 2020, p.1).

Another effort is to shift the tax revenues of large cities to other areas. In 2008, the
15 Japanese government started a hometown tax program. It encourages donations to local governments that are different from the taxpayer's place of residence. With this program, taxpayers can benefit from premium gifts, as well as **deductions** of resident tax and income tax, making the donation worthwhile (Moor, 2021).

20 Finally, there is an idea to provide people in **underpopulated** areas with access to better public services. Since those areas tend to have many senior citizens, medical services are essential, and online consultation can be a solution. Asada et al. (2020) focuses on the fact that doctors are aging as well. With online consultation, neither doctors nor patients will need to travel between their homes and hospitals.
25

In summary, differences in population density create tax disparities between urban and rural areas. Solutions to such imbalances include securing the **labor force**, increasing tax revenues, and improving public services in less populated areas. When the young and the old live comfortably together, we can escape the **vicious cycle**.

> Your Reading Speed: **335** words ÷ _____ seconds × 60 = _____ wpm

References
Asada, K., Mitsutake, R., Hashimoto, S., & Sagimori, H. (2020, September 23). *Impending crisis of aging doctors treating aging patients*. Nikkei Asia.
https://vdata.nikkei.com/en/newsgraphics/aging-society/aged-doctor/
International Labour Organization. (2020, July 16). *Practical guide on teleworking during the COVID-19 pandemic and beyond*.
https://www.ilo.org/travail/info/publications/WCMS_751232/lang--en/index.htm.
Moor, L. (2021, November 9). Furusato nozei: An introduction to Japan's hometown tax program. *Tokyo Weekender*.
https://www.tokyoweekender.com/japan-life/furusato-nozei-japan-hometown-tax/

1. **Choose the phrase that is related to each word / phrase.**

    1. vicious cycle ( )
    2. disparity ( )
    3. deduction ( )
    4. underpopulated ( )
    5. labor force ( )

    (a) a difference or gap between two things
    (b) a repeating pattern of negative events
    (c) having fewer people than ideal
    (d) taking away an amount from a total
    (e) working population

2. **Read the passage and choose the best answer to each question.**

    1. What will happen in depopulated areas when many young people move to cities?
    (A) There will be increased job opportunities.
    (B) The learning environment will improve.
    (C) There will be insufficient local tax revenue.
    (D) Public services will be improved.

    2. Which solution is introduced as the first example?
    (A) Encouraging young people to move to large cities.
    (B) Providing insufficient public services.
    (C) Encouraging workers to stay in rural areas.
    (D) Allowing employees to work only from their offices.

    3. What is Moor's (2021) stance on the hometown tax program?
    (A) It needs too much effort from taxpayers.
    (B) It should be banned by the government.
    (C) It is different from the taxpayers' expectations.
    (D) It offers various benefits to taxpayers.

    4. What does the article by Asada et al. (2020) suggest?
    (A) Hiring more doctors in underpopulated areas.
    (B) Building more hospitals to give better services.
    (C) Providing online consultation services.
    (D) Providing transportation for patients.

    5. Which of the following is one of the solutions discussed in the article?
    (A) Keeping the labor force in populated areas.
    (B) Increasing tax revenues in rural areas.
    (C) Making life easier in large cities.
    (D) Encouraging young people to move to cities.

Writing Tips: *APA (1) Making a reference list*

The reference list comes after your whole essay. It should contain all of the sources you used in the essay, and be in alphabetical order. Copy all the references cited on page 10. Pay attention to punctuation marks and italics.

A _____ .

_____ .

https://vdata.nikkei.com/en/newsgraphics/aging-society/aged-doctor/

I _____

_____ .

https://www.ilo.org/travail/info/publications/WCMS_751232/lang-en/index.htm.

M _____

_____ .

https://www.tokyoweekender.com/japan-life/furusato-nozei-japan-hometown-tax/

Writing Outline: *Problem and solution*

 1-09

Write about one social issue in Japan. What is the problem? What is one solution? Include at least two references.

Introduction	This essay will describe [one social problem] in Japan. I will explain the problem and one possible solution.
Problem	[Problem] is a big problem for Japan. This means....
Solution	One solution is [solution]. This might help because....
Conclusion	To sum up, [problem]. As a solution, [solution].
References	

Personal Safety

身の回りの安全について考えよう

Have you ever felt unsafe on campus?

    a. Yes, all the time.

    b. Yes, sometimes.

    c. Not often.

    d. Never.

> *I chose answer _____ , because .....*
> ....
> ....
> ....

Words in Focus: *Search the internet for words and phrases.*　 1-10

❏ burglary   ❏ emergency

❏ campus escort service   ❏ salmonella

❏ contaminated   ❏ sexual assault

❏ criminal offense   ❏ tap water

❏ diarrhea   ❏ theft

The DO's and DON'Ts of campus safety

While we want to keep the campus safe for everyone, unfortunately, some crimes occur. Look at the pie chart. Here are some criminal offenses that happened last year. To keep yourself out of ☐ 1 ☐ , please read and follow these DO's and DON'Ts of campus life.

On campus…
1) DO make sure you know where the campus emergency phones are.
2) DO use the campus escort service to get home when it's dark.
3) DO be sure someone (i.e., your roommate) knows where you are.
4) DON'T listen to loud music when you're traveling. Be aware of your surroundings.

In your dorm…
1) DON'T keep paperwork with ☐ 2 ☐ information lying on your desk.
2) DON'T keep your door unlocked.
3) DO discuss room rules with your roommate, like who can be invited to the room.
4) DO have a laptop lock on your computer.

At college parties…
1) DO keep your drink with you at ☐ 3 ☐ .
2) DO keep track of how much alcohol you've consumed.
3) DON'T take drinks from other people. Unless there's a server, get your drink yourself.
4) DO plan for how you're going to get home.

For more information, please come to the Campus Safety Seminar, on August 23rd. It will be in Room 101 (Building 2, first floor), and doors will open at 1 pm. We are planning to have a one-hour seminar. You will get free coffee and donuts if you join!

1. Choose the best answer to complete the missing words in the passage.

1. (A) control
   (B) danger
   (C) order
   (D) service

2. (A) general
   (B) historical
   (C) personal
   (D) technical

3. (A) no times
   (B) less times
   (C) more times
   (D) all times

2. Read the passage and choose the best answer to each question.

1. Look at the pie chart. Which of the following statements is true?
   (A) There are twice as many burglaries as sexual assaults.
   (B) The most serious problem on campus is the theft of bicycles.
   (C) Most crimes that occur off campus are not dangerous.
   (D) There have been no reported cases of stalking.

2. What should you do if it's dark on campus, but you want to go home?
   (A) Listen to loud music.
   (B) Call the escort service.
   (C) Buy a laptop lock.
   (D) Run home as fast as you can.

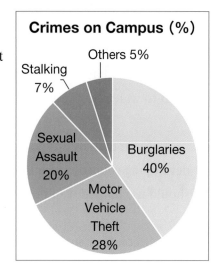

3. What is NOT planned for the seminar on August 23rd?
   (A) It starts in the afternoon.
   (B) It will take at least one hour.
   (C) You can buy lunch.
   (D) You can get free coffee and donuts.

Reading Tips: *Cause and effect*

英文において、cause and effect（原因と結果）はきちんと明記されている場合とそうでない場合があります。後者の場合、想像力を働かせてイメージしながら読むと、すでに持っている知識・仮説をうまく使った英文処理が可能となり、より早く、深く英文の全容を理解できます。前ページの情報について、円グラフに示されている犯罪の被害防止とのつながりを考えてみましょう。以下の表に✓印を入れ、なぜ被害防止につながるか説明しましょう。

	On campus				In your dorm				At college parties			
	1)	2)	3)	4)	1)	2)	3)	4)	1)	2)	3)	4)
Burglaries												
Motor vehicle theft												
Sexual assault												
Stalking												
Others												

Eat and drink safely

Do you like to travel? As a college student, you might be thrilled at the different things you can eat and drink abroad. In a familiar country, staying safe while exploring new food and drink is pretty simple. For example, in Japan, you are probably used to finding safe, clean restaurants, and **tap water** is usually drinkable. In contrast, in some countries, you need to
5 be aware of what to avoid, and **tap water** may not be drinkable. In this essay, we will discuss what to watch out for when you eat and drink in an unfamiliar country.

First, the safest type of drinking water in many countries is bottled water. Especially in developing countries, drinking **tap water** could lead to **diarrhea**. As a safety procedure, you
10 should use bottled water even for brushing your teeth.

Second, when you drink bottled water, also make sure that the bottle has not been opened before or **tampered** with. In some countries, dishonest vendors have created "fake" bottled water from reused bottles. Also, when eating out, avoid water with ice. This is because
15 the ice cubes could be made from contaminated **tap water**.

Third, when eating, do not eat anything raw, or half-cooked. For example, you should avoid raw vegetables that could have been washed with **tap water**. Also, do you like eating raw eggs over rice? We can eat eggs raw in Japan because there is a careful procedure to clean the
20 eggs. Unfortunately, eggs are not made to be consumed raw in many countries. That is, the eggs aren't cleaned, which means that they may have **germs** like salmonella. To be on the safe side, you should eat fully cooked eggs outside of Japan.

In conclusion, being safe about what you drink and eat is very important. Try to
25 be aware of where your food and drink come from. It is also useful if you look up more information about food and drink safety for the country you're visiting. It is only then that you can fully enjoy your **culinary** adventure abroad!

Your Reading Speed: **347** words ÷ _____ seconds × 60 = _____ wpm

1. Choose the phrase that is related to each word / phrase.

1. tap water   (   )
2. diarrhea   (   )
3. tamper   (   )
4. germ   (   )
5. culinary   (   )

> **(a)** a stomach problem
> **(b)** a virus, disease or bacteria
> **(c)** related to cooking or the kitchen
> **(d)** to damage something
> **(e)** water that is supplied to homes and workplaces

2. Read the passage and choose the best answer to each question.

1. Why is it easy to keep safe while exploring new food in Japan?
   (A) Because you know how to find safe restaurants.
   (B) Because tap water is not good for drinking.
   (C) Because everyone uses bottled water.
   (D) Because everyone has different ideas about "cleanliness."

2. What is recommended in paragraph 2?
   (A) Visiting many different countries.
   (B) Going to developed countries.
   (C) Drinking tap water.
   (D) Brushing teeth with bottled water.

3. Why are some vendors "dishonest"?
   (A) Because they sell illegal ice water.
   (B) Because they sell illegal hot water.
   (C) Because they reuse old bottles to make new water bottles.
   (D) Because they reuse old tap water to make new tap water.

4. Why should you avoid eating raw eggs outside of Japan?
   (A) Because they are expensive.
   (B) Because they are washed with tap water.
   (C) Because they are not cleaned like eggs in Japan.
   (D) Because they are illegal.

5. In the end, what does the author recommend you do?
   (A) Search for more information.
   (B) Save people suffering from diarrhea.
   (C) Wash your vegetables every day.
   (D) Eat only fully-cooked eggs in Japan.

The passage on page 16 is an example of formal writing. Now, see the table below. The right side of the table shows some of the messages rewritten in an informal way. Try finding which part of the passage each "informal" LINE message corresponds to.

Formal (Eat and drink safely)	Informal (LINE message)
First, the _____ _____ _____ _____ _____ _____ _____ _____ _____ _____ _____ _____ .	Bottled water is best! :)
Especially in _____ _____ , _____ _____ _____ _____ _____ _____ _____ .	BTW, drinking tap water in developing countries can make your stomach hurt.
Also, when _____ _____ , _____ _____ _____ _____ .	Ice water? BAD idea.

 1-13

Write a formal essay about one problem with personal safety for students. What is one cause of this problem? What is one effect?

Introduction	One problem that students may experience with personal safety is.... This can be caused by [cause] and results in [effect].
Cause	One of the main causes of [problem] is....
Effect	One effect of [problem] is....
Conclusion	Due to [cause], [effect]. Thus, students should [advice].

Gender

社会的性差について考えよう

Warm-up: *Share your ideas.*

Do you think men and women have equal opportunities in Japan?

a. Yes, definitely.

b. Yes, somewhat.

c. Not really.

d. Not at all.

I chose answer _____ , because .....

....

....

....

Words in Focus: *Search the internet for words and phrases.* 1-14

❏ CEO

❏ evidence

❏ gay marriage

❏ the Gender Gap Report

❏ Leo Varadkar

❏ the LGBTQ+ movement

❏ nursery care

❏ rainbow parade

❏ sexuality

❏ the World Economic Forum

Join us in the rainbow parade!

Calling all supporters of the LGBTQ+ movement! Are you out and proud? Curious about your sexuality? Or a heterosexual ally? Join in the parade at Dublin Pride. This year, it will be held on Saturday, September 21st.

In 2001, the Netherlands became the first country in the world to accept same-sex marriage. By the mid-2020s, more than 30 countries had followed. Many of these countries were in Europe or the Americas. Here in Ireland, gay marriage was introduced in 2015 after 62% of people ☐ **1** ☐ it in a public vote. By June 2017, 1 million US citizens were in same-sex marriages. These included the actors Jodie Foster and George Takei. In the same year, Leo Varadkar, who is homosexual, became Prime Minister of Ireland.

Same-sex relationships ☐ **2** ☐ illegal in many countries in the past. Later, couples became free to have relationships. People celebrated with street parties as laws were changed. On the other hand, LGBTQ+ acts are still punished by death in more than ten countries, including Qatar, the 2022 Football World Cup host.

The introduction of same-sex marriage laws shows that attitudes to marriage are changing in the 21st century. While more countries are likely to follow this Western trend, others may refuse to change. The move towards granting equal rights to humans may progress, but ☐ **3** ☐ shows that there will be some delays along the way. Come along to Dublin LGBTQ+ Pride on September 21st to show your support!

Related articles

Rights for LGBTQ+ people in selected countries (2023)
◇ **Countries accepting marriage**
 USA
 Ireland
 Taiwan
◇ **Countries accepting LGBTQ+ acts but not marriage**
 Japan
 Vietnam
 Peru
◇ **Countries punishing LGBTQ+ acts**
 UAE
 Iran
 Jamaica

1. **Choose the best answer to complete the missing words in the passage.**

1. (A) backed
(B) denied
(C) opposed
(D) rejected

2. (A) are
(B) had been
(C) has been
(D) will be

3. (A) confidence
(B) dependence
(C) evidence
(D) guidance

2. **Read the passage and choose the best answer to each question.**

1. Which of the following events happened most recently?

   (A) The Netherlands allowed same-sex marriage.

   (B) 62% of Irish people took part in a vote.

   (C) Ireland allowed same-sex marriage.

   (D) Ireland elected a gay leader.

2. According to this passage, what is the future for same-sex marriage?

   (A) More countries will allow it.   (B) Fewer countries will allow it.

   (C) No countries will allow it.   (D) All countries will allow it.

3. Look at the list of related articles. Which of the following are options for wedding ceremony locations for an LGBTQ+ couple?

   (A) In the USA, but not in Japan.   (B) Either Ireland or Iran.

   (C) Either Taiwan or Vietnam.   (D) In Peru, but not in the UAE.

Reading Tips: *Understanding timelines*

文章の内容を素早く把握するために、そこに書かれている時系列の情報 (timeline) を整理する手法があります。下記の表を使って、前ページ第2段落にある出来事が何年に起こったか (起こる予定なのか) を整理しましょう。

	Events	Year
1	Join in the _____ _____ _____ _____. _____ _____, it will be held on Saturday, September 21st.	this year
2	In _____, _____ _____ _____ _____ _____ _____ in the world to accept same-sex marriage.	
2	By the mid-_____, _____ _____ _____ _____ _____ _____.	by
2	Here in _____, gay marriage _____ _____ _____ _____....	
2	By June _____, 1 million _____ _____ _____ _____ _____-_____ _____.	
3	..., including _____, _____ _____ _____ _____ _____.	
4	Come along to _____ _____ _____ on September 21st to show your support!	

The Gender Gap Report

The Gender Gap Report is produced annually by the World Economic Forum. It ranks around 150 countries by gender **equality**. The report focuses on health, education, economy, and **politics**. In 2020, Iceland was the top-ranked country, with a score of 0.877. "Zero" represents total inequality, and "1" represents total **equality**. The lowest-ranked country was
5　Yemen, with a score of 0.494. What is it like for women in Iceland, Yemen, and Japan?

In Iceland, female and male students achieve equal levels of success. Furthermore, 40% of government ministers are female. There has been a female leader for 22 of the last 50 years. This is **in contrast with** Yemen, where only 1.6% of companies employ women in senior
10　management. In addition, only 35% of women in Yemen can read or write, compared to 73% of men. These two societies are very different.

Japan's score of 0.652 means that the situation here is closer to Yemen than Iceland. In particular, Japan's rankings in politics and economy are low. For example, almost 95% of
15　senior roles in Japanese companies are held by men. **Additionally**, 77% of senior politicians are male. As a result, Japan was judged to have the greatest gender gap of all developed countries. In 2013, the Prime Minister announced a plan to increase the number of working women. This failed to have an impact on senior management.

20　One problem in Japan is that women do not trust other women to hold senior positions. A survey showed that only 28% of women in Japan feel comfortable with a female CEO of a major company. This compares to 70% of women in the USA. Another problem is that there are not enough childcare places. If children cannot be placed into **nursery care**, their mothers are forced into their traditional role of caregivers.
25

Countries with the smallest gender gap are those where women have similar levels of power to men. Having power in the workplace, **politics** and education allows people to better control their lives. A smaller gender gap enables both men and women to create an equal society, with members who are able to act freely. This should be an aim for all members of
30　society.

> Your Reading Speed: **368** words ÷ _____ seconds × 60 = _____ wpm

Reference
World Economic Forum (2020). *Global gender gap report*. https://www.weforum.org/reports/gender-gap-2020-report-100-years-pay-equality/

1. Choose the phrase that is related to each word / phrase.

1. equality   (   )
2. politics   (   )
3. in contrast with (   )
4. additionally   (   )
5. nursery care   (   )

(a) fairness
(b) furthermore
(c) looking after young children
(d) related to the running of a country
(e) totally different from

2. Read the passage and choose the best answer to each question.

1. Which of the three countries achieved perfect gender equality?
   (A) Iceland.
   (B) Yemen.
   (C) Japan.
   (D) None of the above.

2. Which of the following groups is said to have the greatest gender equality?
   (A) Students from Iceland.
   (B) Company managers in Iceland.
   (C) Managers from Yemen.
   (D) Students from Yemen.

3. What is Japan's ranking in terms of gender equality?
   (A) Higher than Yemen.
   (B) As high as that of Iceland.
   (C) As low as other developed countries.
   (D) The lowest in the world.

4. According to the article, why will it be difficult to increase the number of women in work in Japan?
   (A) Men do not want women to hold senior positions.
   (B) Women prefer to take care of young children.
   (C) Both (A) and (B).
   (D) Neither (A) nor (B).

5. What is the benefit of having a smaller gender gap?
   (A) Men can control women's lives.
   (B) Politicians can have more power in society.
   (C) Women can have more power than men.
   (D) People are more likely to control their own lives.

Writing Tips: *Different types of transitions*

Transitions are the words/phrases you can use to clearly connect your ideas. Find some examples of transitions from the passage on page 22. Then, think about how each of these transitions are being used.

Transitions	How they are used in "The Gender Gap Report."
Furthermore	Furthermore, 40% of _____ _____ _____ _____ .
In contrast	This is in contrast with _____ , where only _____ _____ _____ _____ _____ _____ _____ _____ .
As a result	As a result, Japan was _____ _____ _____ _____ _____ _____ _____ _____ _____ _____ .

Writing Outline: *Following timelines* 1-17

How have attitudes to gender changed in your country, or another country? Write about three eras (including today) with different attitudes.

Introduction	Attitudes to gender are changing in many parts of the world. I will look at how this has changed in [country], with reference to [era 1], [era 2], and today.
Era 1	To begin with, in [era 1],....
Era 2	Later on, in [era 2],....
Today	In current times,....
Conclusion	Therefore, attitudes (do not) seem to have changed from [era 1] to today. In the future [prediction].

UNIT 5

Religion

世界の宗教について考えよう

Warm-up: *Share your ideas.*

What do you say when greeting someone at Christmas?

a. Merry Christmas.

b. Happy Holidays.

c. Something else.

d. Nothing.

I chose answer _____ , because .....

....

....

....

Words in Focus: *Search the internet for words and phrases.*

❏ Christianity

❏ etiquette

❏ Hanukkah

❏ Hinduism

❏ Holy Communion

❏ Islam

❏ Jesus Christ

❏ Judaism

❏ Rosh Hashanah

❏ Taoism

Holiday Etiquette Tips

It's December 24th. People are about to enjoy a week or two off work or school. Decorations are displayed. Presents have been bought and wrapped. Special food and drinks are ready to be cooked and eaten. The last thing to do before finishing work for the holiday is to say... what?

Check out these seasonal greetings tips!

"Merry Christmas"
For many people, this season is a Christian holiday. Christians believe that December 25th is a celebration of the birth of the son of their God. In the USA, 78% of people are Christian.

"Happy Holidays"
For Jewish people, December means Hanukkah, the "Festival of Light." Therefore, using a neutral phrase such as "Happy Holidays" (with a plural "s") sends good wishes to people without the danger of [1] them.

Which phrase should I use?
It can be difficult to know what to say in modern Western society. One key [2] is to open your mind to all members of society. Listen to what they say, ask them if you are not sure, and respect their beliefs. This will make them more respectful of your beliefs too. Modern societies can be [3] when members of a population from different backgrounds understand each other. This means that we can all have very Happy Holidays, and a Merry Christmas too.

1. **Choose the best answer to complete the missing words in the passage.**

1. (A) an upset   **2.** (A) principle   **3.** (A) damaged
     (B) to upset   (B) practical   (B) enriched
     (C) the upset   (C) particle   (C) harmful
     (D) upsetting   (D) participle   (D) illegal

2. **Read the passage and choose the best answer to each question.**

1. Which of the following do people NOT regularly do before Christmas?
   (A) Decorate their homes.
   (B) Buy and wrap presents.
   (C) Go out to eat special food.
   (D) Exchange seasonal greetings.

2. How does the writer recommend greeting people?
   (A) With "Happy Holidays."
   (B) With "Merry Christmas."
   (C) However you like.
   (D) However they like.

3. Look at the cards on the previous page. Which one is especially designed for Jewish people?
   (A) The one on the left.
   (B) The one in the middle.
   (C) The one on the right.
   (D) None of the above.

Reading Tips: *Similarities and differences*

文中で述べられている事象を similarities (類似点) と differences (相違点) で仕分けすると効率よく情報整理ができます。Christian と Jewish で行われるお祝いイベントについて、前ページの文章から情報を抜き出して下の表に書き、比較しましょう。

	Christian	Jewish
Month	_____	_____
Name of the event	_____	_____ (____ " _____ ____ _____ ")
What to say during the event	_____ _____	_____ _____

Food customs of world religions

Although there are many disagreements among the religions of the world, they can all agree on the importance of food. They each have their own foods which they use to **mark** important events, and in many cases there are foods which members are not able to eat. This essay will give some examples, by considering some of the world's major religions, including
5 Christianity (31% of the global population), Islam (23%), Hinduism (15%), Judaism (0.2%), and others such as Taoism.

It is important to understand why food is important to each **celebration**. First, Christian people regularly take part in a ceremony known as "Holy Communion." This involves
10 eating bread and drinking wine. The bread represents the body of Jesus and the wine is his blood. Second, Jewish people eat apples and honey to celebrate the new year festival "Rosh Hashanah" (which is **marked** in September). They believe that eating these will lead to a sweet new year. In China, followers of Taoism eat noodles for new year. This indicates that they will have a long life. It can be hard for many people to imagine these events without their key
15 foods.

In addition, religions sometimes give strict rules to their believers about what they cannot eat. Followers of Islam are forbidden to eat pork. Some other meats are only permitted if the animal is killed without causing too much pain. Hindus do not eat beef as the
20 cow is a sacred animal in Hinduism. Many of them also choose not to eat meat or fish. This is to avoid causing **harm** to animals.

Some **restrictions** on food are limited to certain times of the year. For example, Roman Catholic Christians traditionally do not eat meat on Fridays during Lent, which is a period of
25 40 days before Easter. Many of them tend to eat fish instead. Jesus Christ died on a Friday, so avoiding meat on this day is out of respect. Learning the reasons for these food habits helps to promote an understanding of the religion.

Religious customs are often many hundreds of years old so it can be difficult to trace
30 their origins. In addition, customs change with time and place. Therefore, not all of the customs described here are true for all followers of a religion. Some believers follow teachings **strictly**. Others are more open to changing their habits. Understanding other religions can lead to a more peaceful world, and a brighter future.

Your Reading Speed: **410** words ÷ _____ seconds × 60 = _____ wpm

1. Choose the phrase that is related to each word / phrase.

1. mark   (   )   **(a)** a limit
2. celebration   (   )   **(b)** a special occasion
3. harm   (   )   **(c)** pain
4. restriction   (   )   **(d)** severely
5. strictly   (   )   **(e)** to observe an event

2. Read the passage and choose the best answer to each question.

1. What is the main idea of this essay?
    (A) Food is an important part of religious festivals.
    (B) There are many foods which religious people must eat daily.
    (C) Festival foods in most religions are similar.
    (D) Understanding the meaning of each food is very difficult.

2. Which of these is a correct explanation of religious festival food?
    (A) Bread and wine have special meanings for Jewish people.
    (B) Eating sweets in January brings a sweet year to Christians.
    (C) Members of the Taoist religion eat noodles for new year.
    (D) None of the above.

3. Which animals are not eaten by followers of 1) Hinduism and 2) Islam?
    (A) 1) Pigs and 2) fish.
    (B) 1) Cows and 2) pigs.
    (C) 1) Fish and 2) sheep.
    (D) 1) Sheep and 2) cows.

4. When do Roman Catholic Chistians traditionally avoid eating meat?
    (A) Fridays all year round.
    (B) Certain days during Lent.
    (C) During Easter.
    (D) On Jesus' birthday.

5. Which of the following statements is the writer likely to disagree with?
    (A) Religious customs change with time and place.
    (B) It is better not to eat pork because many religious people cannot eat it.
    (C) Understanding the reasons for religious customs is helpful.
    (D) People with different backgrounds can learn a lot from each other.

Writing Tips: *Descriptive essay*

When you write a descriptive essay, you try to describe things, such as a person, place, object, emotions, experience, and so on. It is important to describe using your five senses (taste, smell, touch, sight, hearing). For the paragraph below, write down which phrase ((1) ~ (5)) describes which of the five senses.

> I will write about how my family celebrated Christmas when I was a little kid. On Christmas day, I woke up to the sound of my mother's cooking: boiling water, (1) the oven humming, and the frying pan hissing. I couldn't wait to enjoy the (2) sweet or salty dishes she was preparing. There was also a slight (3) spicy aroma. I jumped out of my bed with excitement. I instantly saw (4) a box in red, shiny gift wrapping! I ripped off the wrapping, to find a (5) soft, furry teddy bear inside.

Write down which of the five senses each phrase is describing.
(taste, smell, touch, sight, hearing)

(1)   (2)   (3)   (4)   (5)

Writing Outline: *Similarities and differences*

 1-21

Describe two different religions. In what ways are they similar and different? Include at least two references.

Introduction	There are many religions in the world, including [religion 1] and [religion 2]. These two religions are similar in [similarities], but different in [differences].
Similarities	One similarity of [religion 1] and [religion 2] is.... In addition,....
Differences	One difference between [religion 1] and [religion 2] is.... On the other hand,....
Conclusion	In conclusion, followers of [religion 1] and [religion 2] may be able to agree when it comes to [similarities]. However, they may struggle when it comes to [differences] because....
References	

Business

国際ビジネスについて考えよう

Warm-up: *Share your ideas.*

Which of the following economic activities are you most interested in?

- **a.** Harvesting natural resources.
- **b.** Processing raw materials.
- **c.** Providing services.
- **d.** Other economic activities.

> *I chose answer _____ , because .....*
> ....
> ....
> ....

Words in Focus: *Search the internet for words and phrases.* 1-22

- ❏ advertisement
- ❏ aptitude
- ❏ hashtag
- ❏ influencer
- ❏ job hunting

- ❏ manufacturing
- ❏ NGO
- ❏ social media marketing
- ❏ tertiary
- ❏ three-sector economy model

What sector would you like to work in?

The first step in job hunting is to think about what kind of field can make the most of your aptitude. Economies can be divided into sectors. The three-sector model was developed in the early 20th century. Here, let's take a look at the original model.

Primary sector	Secondary sector	Tertiary sector
Raw materials	**Manufacturing**	**Service**
This sector includes industries involved in <u>raw material</u> extraction and production.	This sector includes industries that <u>manufacture</u> finished, ⬚ 2 products or that are involved in <u>construction</u>.	This sector includes providing <u>services</u> to other businesses and final consumers.
Examples are …	**Examples are …**	**Examples are …**
agriculture	textile production	transportation
logging	automobile manufacturing	sales
⬚ 1	handicrafts	food service
forestry	chemical engineering	entertainment
mining	construction	health and social work

Later, some economists expanded the model by adding the fourth and fifth sectors. For example, a group of researchers suggested that the service sector be divided into two: urbanization and control sectors. In addition to the three-sector model, others regard information-based or knowledge-oriented industries as the fourth sector. Moreover, there are models that categorize non-profit work, such as charities and NGOs, into the fourth sector.

As people's lifestyles change, so do the key industries they need. Imagine yourself in the future. In which industry will you ⬚ 3 demonstrate your strength the most?

1. **Choose the best answer to complete the missing words in the passage.**

1. (A) education	**2.** (A) usable	**3.** (A) be able to
(B) entertainment	(B) use	(B) be aware of
(C) fishing	(C) used	(C) be fond of
(D) information	(D) using	(D) be interested in

2. Read the passage and choose the best answer to each question.

1. What is the three-sector model?
   (A) A model of economic development.
   (B) A model of job hunting.
   (C) A model of sector division.
   (D) A model of aptitude testing.

2. Look at the job advertisement. What sector is this business related to?
   (A) The primary sector.
   (B) The secondary sector.
   (C) The manufacturing sector.
   (D) The tertiary sector.

NOW HIRING!
Medical staff

Send your résumé to:
nurses@hospital.com

3. Which of the sectors was added to the three-sector model later?
   (A) The urbanization sector.
   (B) The information-based sector.
   (C) The non-profit sector.
   (D) All of the above.

Reading Tips: *Categorizing*

文章を読んで情報を整理する際に、categorizing という手法が役立ちます。前ページで述べられている4つのセクター分類を見直し、内容を書き出しましょう。

Sector	Three-sector model	New model (1)	New model (2)	New model (3)
Primary	_____ _____			
Secondary	_____			
Tertiary	_____	_____ _____ _____	_____	_____
Fourth			_ _____ _____	_ _____

1-24

What are types of social media marketing?

Have you ever heard the phrase "social media marketing"? It is basically a type of digital marketing. You have probably seen this in **advertisements** online. Or perhaps, your favorite celebrity often advertises some cool gadgets on their channel. Here, we will describe three types of social media marketing: influencer marketing, paid media marketing, and
5 content marketing.

The first type of marketing is called influencer marketing. An "influencer" in social media is a person who has many followers. The followers often serve as an audience for whatever the influencer posts. In influencer marketing, the company asks the influencer to
10 introduce their products to an audience. The advantage here is that since the influencer's audience is large and **loyal**, there is a high possibility the audience will be convinced to buy the product. The influencer can also explain details about the product like this in their live streaming: "Hey! Listen up! This lipstick is awesome. It never comes off!"

15 The second type of marketing is called paid media marketing. Here, companies ask a paid placement agency to put their product **advertisements** on social media. For example, many users can see some **advertisements** for **cosmetics** as they scroll through posts. The main drawback is that companies often need to pay a lot of money in order to place their **advertisements**. However, the advantages are great too. Companies using paid media
20 marketing can expect a wide range of people to see their **advertisement**. The company can also control the content of the advertisement.

The third and final type of marketing is called content marketing. With this method, companies make and post some "content" like blogs, pictures, and videos on their own social
25 media account. To be effective, the content needs to be **straightforward** and logical. For example, say Company A is selling a product that can take great pictures. Then, the same company has a website where users of this product can upload their pictures and show them to others. This is a good place to do content marketing, because many users are interested in how well their pictures show up. It's also easy to find similar content; users simply have to
30 find other pictures using the hashtag #CompanyA.

In conclusion, we have introduced three types of social media marketing. It is important to note that none of these three types is the "best" way to sell products. In the end, the company needs to decide the type of marketing that can clearly show the **selling points** of their
35 product.

Your Reading Speed: **422** words ÷ _____ seconds × 60 = _____ wpm

1. Choose the phrase that is related to each word / phrase.

1. advertisement ( )
2. loyal ( )
3. cosmetics ( )
4. straightforward ( )
5. selling point ( )

(a) easy to do or understand
(b) feature of a product that makes it attractive
(c) giving or showing firm and constant support
(d) something that promotes a product, event, or job
(e) substances that you put on your face or body

2. Read the passage and choose the best answer to each question.

1. What is one example of "social media marketing" ?
(A) You see a sports drink advertisement in a newspaper.
(B) You see a museum advertisement on a bus.
(C) A YouTuber advertises eyeshadow on their channel.
(D) A movie star advertises some clothes in a magazine.

2. Who is described as an "influencer" in social media?
(A) Somebody who never uses social media.
(B) Somebody who serves as an audience.
(C) Somebody who has many followers.
(D) Somebody who makes lipstick.

3. What is one problem with paid media marketing?
(A) Many people see the advertisement.
(B) Many people don't click on the advertisement.
(C) Companies have to pay a lot.
(D) Companies have to employ more people.

4. What is NOT one example of content marketing?
(A) A picture.
(B) A blog post.
(C) A video.
(D) A letter.

5. What does the author conclude at the end?
(A) Influencer marketing is difficult.
(B) Paid media marketing is the most successful.
(C) Content marketing is the least successful.
(D) The best marketing style depends on the company.

There are many differences between written and spoken English. In the chart below, find each phrase from the passage on page 34 and compare the two styles.

Written	Spoken
Here, we will describe three types of social media marketing: _____ _____, _____ _____ _____, ____ _____ _____.	I'm talking about social media marketing. I'm gonna show you three types. They are like, influencer marketing, paid media marketing, and content marketing.
It is notable that this lipstick does not come off easily, which is an excellent feature.	____! _____ ____! This lipstick is _____. It _____ _____ ____!
Here, companies ask a _____ _____ _____ ____ ____ _____ _____ _____ ____ _____ _____.	So, you know those agencies that handle ads on social media? Yeah, so, you can pay'em and ask'em to post ads for your products.

Writing Outline: *Categorizing*

 1-25

Choose three "example" industries from the graphic on page 32. Write a blog post that explains what is special about each industry and include the names of example companies.

Introduction	There are many different kinds of business in the world. Let's look at [category 1], [category 2] and [category 3].
Category 1	[Category 1] is....
Category 2	As for [category 2],.....
Category 3	Meanwhile, [category 3] is....
Conclusion	Now you know a bit about [categories 1, 2 and 3]. Comment on any other business categories you know.

Career

キャリア形成について考えよう

Warm-up: *Share your ideas.*

What is your main concern when applying for a job?

a. Salary and benefits.

b. Working conditions.

c. Chances of promotion.

d. The job description.

> *I chose answer _____, because .....*
> ....
> ....
> ....

Words in Focus: *Search the internet for words and phrases.* 2-01

❑ available upon request

❑ career plan

❑ chronological order

❑ competitive salary

❑ CV

❑ internship

❑ qualification

❑ varieties and styles of English

❑ volunteer

❑ work-life balance

Ken Yamamoto

Home address:
Minato 1-1-3, Minami-ku, Kobe, Hyogo, 650-8586

Mobile phone:
+81-90-1111-1111

Email address:
ken_yamamoto@u.japan.ac.jp

Career Focus

To pursue a career in the area of customer service by using my proficiency in languages, knowledge of economics, and skills in interpersonal communication for mutual growth.

Profile

• BA in Economics • Qualification of Bookkeeping Level 2	▶ High 1 for business operations
• Award for the Champion of English Speech Contest • TOEIC 850 (certified recent score available upon request)	▶ 2 in Japanese and English
• Customer-oriented work experience in a convenience store, as well as in the hospitality industry	▶ Skilled in customer service
• Internship experience in a leading international company • Volunteer experience in an academic institution	▶ Flexible in a team environment

Work/Training Experiences

July–September 2024: Internship experience at AAA Company Ltd.
Assisted with a project focused on 3 business operations abroad.
2023–present: Volunteer at the International Relations office, ABC University
Aid international students with class registration and coursework.
2022–2023: Part-time clerk at a convenience store
Provided customer service in both Japanese and English.
Organized shelves, monitored inventory, and trained new staff.
2021–2022: Part-time position as a cleaning staff member at YYY Hotel
Responsible for making beds, cleaning rooms, and managing amenity inventory.

1. Choose the best answer to complete the missing words in the passage.

1.	2.	3.
(A) essential	(A) Fluent	(A) expand
(B) initial	(B) Fluid	(B) expanding
(C) partial	(C) Fruity	(C) expanded
(D) potential	(D) Frustrate	(D) expansion

2. Read the passage and choose the best answer to each question.

1. What is Ken's career goal?
   (A) To become a language teacher.
   (B) To work in the field of science.
   (C) To work in customer service.
   (D) To become a writer.

2. Which of these experiences did Ken NOT have?
   (A) Internship at a company.
   (B) Volunteering at a university.
   (C) Part-time car sales.
   (D) Part-time job as a cleaner at a hotel.

3. Look at the advertisement. Which of the four requirements might Ken struggle to meet?
   (A) Requirement 1.
   (B) Requirement 2.
   (C) Requirement 3.
   (D) Requirement 4.

> **Recruiting Sales Experts in our Overseas Office!**
>
> **Job details:** You will be hired on a two-year contract at a competitive salary at one of our 24 offices located in 16 different countries.
>
> **Requirements:**
> 1. Proficiency in English and at least one other language.
> 2. Excellent communication skills, with experience of customer service.
> 3. Minimum of three years experience as a sales representative.
> 4. Comfortable with working as part of a team.

Reading Tips: *Sequencing*

英文の中で順序や時系列が入り組んでいる場合、整理して並べ替えることで事象の把握がスムーズになります。これを sequencing といいます。前ページの英文履歴書中の業務経験（work/training experiences）は、直近のものから順に示されています。この業務経験を古い順に並べ替え、ケンの profile とどのように関係するか、まとめましょう。

Year	Experience	Profile
20＿＿ –	Part-time position as a cleaning staff member at ＿＿＿ ＿＿＿	＿＿＿＿-＿＿＿＿ ＿＿＿ ＿＿＿ in a
20＿＿ –	Part-time clerk at a ＿＿＿＿ ＿＿＿	＿＿＿＿ ＿＿＿, as well as in the ＿＿＿ ＿＿＿
20＿＿ –	Volunteer at the International Relations office, ＿＿＿ ＿＿＿	＿＿＿ ＿＿＿ in an ＿＿＿ ＿＿＿
20＿＿	＿＿＿ ＿＿＿ at ＿＿＿ ＿＿＿ Ltd.	Internship experience in a ＿＿＿ ＿＿＿ ＿＿＿

Ken's narrative essay

Ever since I was a child, my grandmother has been telling me to study English so that I can get a good job. Following her advice, I have been learning English for 15 years. I have no difficulty in everyday conversation in English now. So, why did my grandmother think I would get a good job if I studied English? In this essay, I will share three experiences that have
5 influenced my **perspective**.

Before entering college, I had no clear goals. I simply wanted to graduate within four years. However, Jessie, an exchange student from the US, said, "Don't you think you'll waste money if you don't study hard?" This was a new idea to me. **Initially**, I just wanted to have
10 fun with my friends. Then, in May, I started feeling uncomfortable spending time with certain friends. After some time, I met Lily. She helped me realize that college life should be about preparing for the future.

I managed to get through the first semester. I went to New Zealand for a study abroad
15 program during the summer. The English they spoke was different from what I had learned in Japan. One day, I told Ruby, one of my friends in New Zealand, that her English was **weird**. She answered, "That's how we speak in New Zealand." This made me think that I needed to learn varieties and styles of English that would be useful for communicating with people worldwide.
20

After the summer vacation, students started talking about their career plans. Sofia, my friend from Brazil, was serious about work-life balance. Asha from India was mapping out her strategy for marketing herself to Japanese companies. On the other hand, the only thing I had in mind was to get hired somewhere and learn whatever they would teach me. Sofia
25 and Asha pointed out that I was too **naive** to think the company would teach me anything. Though I had a vague vision of myself communicating in English at work, they told me that my contribution to the company was more important than just speaking English.

Looking back on my student life so far, through conversations with my friends, I
30 encountered new ideas. These views were different from what is considered common in Japan. I was able to learn them because I could communicate in English. After all, learning English will not get me a job. Rather, by having various experiences through my language ability, I can think more **flexibly** and, as a result, become the kind of person that companies want.

Your Reading Speed: **425** words ÷ _____ seconds × 60 = _____ wpm

1. **Choose the phrase that is related to each word / phrase.**

1. perspective   (   )
2. initially   (   )
3. weird   (   )
4. naive   (   )
5. flexibly   (   )

> **(a)** a point of view or outlook
> **(b)** able to adjust or adapt easily
> **(c)** at first
> **(d)** innocent or inexperienced
> **(e)** strange or unusual

2. **Read the passage and choose the best answer to each question.**

1. Why did Ken study English?
    (A) Because his grandmother taught him English.
    (B) Because his grandmother recommended it to him.
    (C) Because his grandmother's first language is English.
    (D) Because he wanted to teach English to his grandmother.

2. What was the new idea for Ken?
    (A) Not to have clear goals.
    (B) To graduate from university in four years.
    (C) Not studying hard means losing money.
    (D) Having fun with friends.

3. What did Ken learn in New Zealand?
    (A) How to complete the first semester.
    (B) The ways New Zealanders speak English.
    (C) How to teach Japanese in New Zealand.
    (D) The way people travel around the world.

4. What advice did Sofia and Asha give Ken?
    (A) He should think about the balance between work and free time.
    (B) He should work for a Japanese company.
    (C) He should study English communication more.
    (D) He should think of ways to contribute to the company.

5. How did Ken find his English ability useful?
    (A) To explain the common views of Japan.
    (B) To find a company that pays well.
    (C) To acquire a flexible way of thinking.
    (D) To start a company with his friends.

In a narrative essay, you write about how an event happened in chronological order. The writer focuses on what they experienced by including words such as "I" and "my". Using the chart below, summarize how the passage on page 40 is structured.

Catchy Introduction	Ever since I was a child, my _____ _____ _____ _____ _____ _____ _____ _____ _____ _____ _____ _____ _____ _____.
Beginning	Before entering _____, _____ _____ _____ _____ _____.
Middle	I _____ _____ _____ _____ _____ _____ _____ _____.
End	After the _____ _____, _____ _____ _____ _____ _____ _____ _____ _____ _____.
Conclusion	Looking back on _____ _____ _____ _____ _____, through _____ with my friends, I _____ _____ _____.

  2-04

Write an essay about one successful business person. What is their background? How did they become successful? What will they be remembered for?

Introduction	When you think of successful people in the business world, [Person] may come to mind. I will explain her / his background, how she / he became successful, and what she / he will be remembered for.
Background	In her / his early days, [Person]....
Path to success	Later on, when [Person] was _____ years old,....
Legacy	In the future, [Person] will be remembered for....
Summary	In essence, [Person] [background]. Since then, [path to success]. One day, [legacy].

Japanese Culture

日本の文化について考えよう

Warm-up: *Share your ideas.*

Which aspects of Japanese culture would you like to introduce to visitors to Japan?

a. Japanese sports and arts.

b. Seasonal events.

c. Politeness and courtesy.

d. Japanese pop culture.

I chose answer _____ , because .....

....

....

....

Words in Focus: *Search the internet for words and phrases.*   2-05

❏ accommodation

❏ Japanese tea ceremony

❏ manga

❏ *omotenashi*

❏ one-sided

❏ philosophy

❏ Sen no Rikyu

❏ speech bubble

❏ subtle

❏ technique

How to read manga

1. How to read traditional Japanese manga.

In traditional Japanese manga, the text is written vertically. You read it from top to bottom, right to left. The manga book is bound on the right side. This way it is easier for your eyes to move from right to left. You start with the [1] page, then read the left page, and the next page is on the back of the left page. Within a page, you look at the panels from right to left, and top to bottom.

2. Manga translated into English.

As manga became popular around the world, many were translated into English. In most cases, the words in the speech bubbles were replaced with English, but the pictures remained the [2]. There is a technique for flipping the left and right pages, but it would make most of the characters left-handed. Also, imagine what a clock would look like when it's flipped!

3. Get used to it!

English text is read from left to right. It means, within the speech bubble, your eyes move from left to right. Now, here is a little problem with manga translated into English. Imagine your eye movements. You open a manga. Remember, the first page starts on the right. You look at the picture in the upper right panel of the first page. You read the text in the bubble from left to right. When you finish reading the text, your eyes are probably on the right edge of the page. But now, you need to jump to the panel on the left. Your eyes move from left to right as you read the text in the bubble again, and then find which panel to go to. It's a bit [3] for beginners, but you'll get used to it.

1. Choose the best answer to complete the missing words in the passage.

1. (A) bottom
(B) left
(C) right
(D) upper

2. (A) different
(B) English
(C) Japanese
(D) same

3. (A) confuse
(B) confused
(C) confuses
(D) confusing

2. Read the passage and choose the best answer to each question.

1. How do you read traditional Japanese manga?
   (A) From left to right, top to bottom.
   (B) From right to left, top to bottom.
   (C) From left to right, bottom to top.
   (D) From right to left, bottom to top.

2. Look at the picture of a clock. What is this about?
   (A) Binding the book on the right side.
   (B) Moving your eyes from right to left.
   (C) Splitting the panels in one page.
   (D) Flipping the left and right pages.

3. When do your eyes move from left to right?
   (A) When searching for a good manga to read.
   (B) When turning the pages of Japanese manga.
   (C) When moving to the next panel within a page.
   (D) When reading a speech bubble in English.

Reading Tips: *Comparison and contrast*

複数のものを比較して類似点や相違点を分析することは comparison、対比して相違点を明確にすることは contrast と呼ばれます。比較や対比しながら英文を整理することにより、筆者の意図がより深く理解できます。前ページの文章を元にして、日本語と英語の書式や製本の類似点や相違点をまとめましょう。

	Japanese	English
The text is written...	_____	horizontally
You read it from...	_____ _____ _____ , _____ _____ _____	_____ _____ _____ , _____ _____ _____
The book is bound on...	_____ _____ _____	_____ _____ _____
The first page starts on...	_____ _____	_____ _____

The philosophy behind Japanese hospitality

Have you ever heard of the word *omotenashi*? In English, this word is translated as "Japanese **hospitality**." However, omotenashi and the Western idea of **hospitality** are quite different. In this essay, I will argue why omotenashi is a concept that is similar but separate from the Western idea of **hospitality**.

5

First of all, in order to explain omotenashi, one needs to know where the concept came from. It is said that omotenashi originated from Sen no Rikyu, a historical figure who had a great influence on the Japanese tea ceremony. Sen no Rikyu's **philosophy** was that the interaction between the host and the guest is a one-time experience. Thus, omotenashi needs

10 to be **tailored to** that particular guest. In addition, the word omotenashi directly translates to *omote* (front) and *nashi* (no), which means that anything served does not have a front or back. It needs to come from the host's heart.

How is this **philosophy** of omotenashi shown? When getting ready for the tea ceremony,

15 the host can take up to a year to prepare the flowers and teaware that will fit the season and guest. All of this preparation is **subtle**; the host does not say, "I prepared all these flowers just for you!" to a guest. Moreover, during the actual tea ceremony, both the host and the guest need to cooperate in order for the omotenashi to be complete. For example, as the host makes the tea, the guest takes some time to appreciate the teaware that the host prepared for them.

20

So, what things set omotenashi apart from Western **hospitality**? One difference is the relationship between the host and guest. In the Western idea of **hospitality**, it is the host that provides the accommodation and care. In other words, the relationship is one-sided. With omotenashi, however, both the host and guest need to cooperate. Even if the guest makes a

25 mistake, it's not a huge problem. Out of respect for the guest, the host will not point out the error. Another difference is the distance between the host and guest. In Western **hospitality**, sometimes becoming friendly and **intimate** with guests is valued, whereas in omotenashi, it's more important to be formal and polite.

30 In conclusion, I argued why omotenashi is a concept different from Western **hospitality**. They differ especially in the relationship and distance between the host and the guest, because they originated from separate **philosophies**. While both are valuable things to know about, one must understand the unique **philosophy** behind omotenashi to fully understand Japanese culture.

Your Reading Speed: **424** words ÷ _____ seconds × 60 = _____ wpm

1. Choose the phrase that is related to each word / phrase.

1. hospitality ( )
2. philosophy ( )
3. tailored to ( )
4. subtle ( )
5. intimate ( )

(a) a theory or attitude that guides behavior
(b) be customized
(c) close or warm personal relationship
(d) not obvious in any way
(e) the act of being friendly and welcoming to guests

2. Read the passage and choose the best answer to each question.

1. The author argues that Western hospitality and Japanese omotenashi are…
   (A) Completely different concepts.
   (B) Both addressing the same concept.
   (C) Similar but separate concepts.
   (D) Similar but from a different age.

2. Which of the following statements is true about omotenashi?
   (A) The concept came from Sen no Rikyu.
   (B) The concept is only applicable to tea ceremonies.
   (C) It works the same for all guests.
   (D) It needs to be done on a weekly basis.

3. What does the host prepare for the tea ceremony?
   (A) A guidebook.
   (B) A lecture about the teaware.
   (C) Flowers that fit the season.
   (D) Ready-made tea.

4. What is true about the Western idea of "hospitality"?
   (A) There is less distance between the host and guest.
   (B) It values friendliness.
   (C) The host arranges the accommodation and care.
   (D) All of the above.

5. What does the author say we must do in order to understand Japanese culture?
   (A) Get to know the philosophy behind omotenashi.
   (B) Identify some problems with omotenashi.
   (C) Eliminate the Western idea of "hospitality" from Japan.
   (D) Become a tea ceremony teacher.

In a persuasive essay, the writer presents an argument, and tries to persuade the reader to agree with that particular argument. In the chart below, summarize how the passage on page 46 is structured.

Explanation of argument	In this essay, I will argue why omotenashi is a concept that is _____ ____ _____ _____ ____ _____ _____ ____ _____ .
Beginning	First of all, in order to explain omotenashi, one needs to know _____ ____ _____ ____ _____ .
Middle	How is this _____ ____ _____ _____ ?
End	So, what things ____ _____ _____ _____ _____ _____ _____ ?
Conclusion (Explain argument again)	In conclusion, I argued why _____ ____ ____ _____ _____ _____ _____ _____ .

Write an essay about one aspect of Japanese culture that you would like to change. What are the traditions of this culture? Why would you like to see this culture change? Provide details.

Introduction	This essay will describe one aspect of Japanese culture which I would like to change. I will explain the traditions of [aspect], and....
Traditions	The Japanese culture of [culture] started _____ . At first,....
Reason	The reason why this culture needs to change is ....
Detail	To be specific,....
Conclusion	To conclude, [traditions]. [Reason].

UNIT 9 Law and Peace

法と平和について考えよう

Warm-up: *Share your ideas.*

What do you think is most essential for world peace?

a. Respect for human rights and dignity.

b. A fair and impartial justice system.

c. Effective and transparent governance.

d. Access to food, shelter, and healthcare.

> *I chose answer _____ , because .....*
> ....
> ....
> ....

Words in Focus: *Search the internet for words and phrases.* 2-09

- ❏ the JSDF
- ❏ Nazi Germany
- ❏ the OHCHR
- ❏ UN PKO
- ❏ the Gulf War

- ❏ the International Bill of Human Rights
- ❏ the UN General Assembly
- ❏ the Universal Declaration of Human Rights
- ❏ the US Declaration of Independence
- ❏ World War II

49

2-10

👍 *Online Opinion Poll* 👎	Nov 3, 09:05 Signed in as: **Ken**

Do you agree or disagree? "Japan should send Self-Defense Force personnel to UN PKO."		
	"YES"	"NO"
Current votes:	14	12
Your vote:	☐	☑

Opinions

Claire Japan also should share a burden, rather than just sending money. Financial support alone is not enough. That's why France sends its troops, despite us having to risk our people's lives.

Ming Bao Definitely YES! I checked the UN website. It seems only a few Japanese contribute to UN PKO, while thousands of Chinese are working there.

Zareb I am from South Sudan, and the JSDF helped us to build roads. The engineering skills of the [**1**] should be used more in UN PKO.

Rawan Japan should contribute to keeping world peace. I am from Kuwait, and we remember that Japan did not send any soldiers and did not help us during the Gulf War.

Ayinabeba If Japan sends their people to UN PKO, there will be no place for our country, Ethiopia. Many Ethiopians join UN PKO, because we need financial support from the UN.

Ken We [**2**] send our Self-Defense Force to a "combat area." It is prohibited by our law of 1992.

Donna I heard that Japan is already contributing to UN PKO by transporting goods and soldiers, including our US soldiers.

Huy Japan doesn't have to send its soldiers to combat areas but can train the PKO soldiers in developing countries. My brother was in the Vietnamese army. He was amazed to see the professional way that the JSDF taught him [**3**] to operate the heavy machines under a UN Project.

1. **Choose the best answer to complete the missing words in the passage.**

1. (A) Gulf War	**2.** (A) aren't	**3.** (A) how
(B) JSDF	(B) can	(B) what
(C) South Sudanese	(C) can't	(C) when
(D) UN PKO	(D) will	(D) who

2. **Read the passage and choose the best answer to each question.**

1. Whose opinion is based on the number of people sent to UN PKO?

   (A) Claire.　　　　　(B) Ming Bao.　　　　(C) Zareb.　　　　　(D) Huy.

2. Who said that it is against the law to send JSDF personnel to UN PKO?

   (A) Ayinabeba.　　　(B) Ken.　　　　　　(C) Donna.　　　　　(D) Huy.

3. Compare the online poll below with the one on the previous page. What happened?

   (A) Thirty hours have passed since the previous page.

   (B) Ken has logged out.

   (C) There is now an equal number of votes for and against.

   (D) More people voted "YES."

👍 Online Opinion Poll 👎		Nov 3, 09:35 Signed in as: Ken
Do you agree or disagree? "Japan should send Self-Defense Force personnel to UN PKO."		
	"YES"	"NO"
Current votes:	55	55

Reading Tips: *Main idea and details (2)*

複数の話者が議論をするとそれぞれの話者が入り組むため、主張したいポイントを整理してはっきりさせる必要があります。前ページで紹介されている議論をもとに、それぞれの話者が賛否を論じている根拠を整理しましょう。

Yes	No
Claire ＿＿＿＿＿ ＿＿＿＿ alone ＿＿＿ ＿＿＿ ＿＿＿＿＿.	**Ayinabeba** …there will be ＿＿＿ ＿＿＿ ＿＿＿ ＿＿＿ ＿＿＿＿, ＿＿＿＿.
Ming Bao It seems ＿＿＿ ＿＿ ＿＿ ＿＿＿＿ ＿＿＿＿ to UN PKO, while ＿＿＿＿ ＿＿ ＿＿＿ ＿＿ ＿＿＿ ＿＿＿.	**Ken** It is ＿＿＿＿＿ ＿＿ ＿＿ ＿＿ of 1992.
Zareb The ＿＿＿＿＿ ＿＿＿ of the ＿＿＿ should be ＿＿＿ ＿＿＿ in UN PKO.	**Donna** I heard that ＿＿＿ ＿＿ ＿＿＿ ＿＿＿＿＿ to UN PKO….
Rawan Japan should ＿＿＿＿ ＿＿ ＿＿＿ ＿＿＿ ＿＿＿＿.	**Huy** Japan doesn't have to send its soldiers to combat areas but ＿＿ ＿＿＿ ＿＿ ＿＿ ＿＿＿ ＿＿ ＿＿＿ ＿＿＿＿.

Human rights before and after the Second World War

"All human beings are born free and equal in **dignity** and rights," says Article 1 of the Universal Declaration of Human Rights (UN General Assembly, 1948). This is a basic idea, and various rules have been created to protect human rights. In this essay, the evolution of movements aimed at protecting individuals' basic rights and freedoms will be discussed in
5 three stages: pre- and post-World War II, and the 21st century.

Before World War II, no other country could have a say in whatever laws one country had about the rights of its people. In America, human rights movements arose through the United States Declaration of Independence, signed in 1776. In France, the French Declaration
10 of the Rights of Man and the Citizen was adopted in 1789. In Nazi Germany (1933-1945), however, Nazi racial laws regarded the Jews as inferior beings. As a result, millions of Jews were murdered in death camps (Stone, 2019). The **genocide** was a huge violation of human rights. Nevertheless, no other states could stop it because it was treated as an internal matter of Germany based on its Nazi laws.
15

World War II made people understand the importance of ensuring peoples' **dignity** and rights on a global level. Thus, Article 1 of the UN Charter was made as a **fundamental** goal. The Universal Declaration of Human Rights, created by the United Nations General Assembly in 1948, was the first legal document that aimed to protect human rights worldwide.
20 Later, two international agreements were passed in 1966: one focusing on civil and political rights, and the other on economic, social, and cultural rights. Together, these three documents make up the International Bill of Human Rights.

To this day, the United Nations has been seeking a system to promote and protect
25 human rights. The Office of the High Commissioner for Human Rights (OHCHR) has worked to "**mainstream** human rights in all areas of work" of the UN (OHCHR, n.d.). They cover development, peace and security, and humanitarian affairs. Today, any human rights violation is no longer an internal matter of a state. It is rather an international concern.

30 All in all, the human rights movements have changed over different phases. Before World War II, **intervention** between nations regarding human rights was not possible. The horrific human rights violations that occurred during the war prompted a recognition that people's **fundamental** rights should be universally protected. The UN has been playing a significant role in making human rights a universal issue so that people can live more
35 peacefully and equally to this day.

Your Reading Speed: **432** words ÷ _____ seconds × 60 = _____ wpm

References
The Office of the High Commissioner for Human Rights. (n.d.). *Mainstreaming human rights*.
    https://www.ohchr.org/EN/newyork/Pages/MainstreamingHR.aspx
Stone, L. (2019). Quantifying the Holocaust: Hyperintense kill rates during the Nazi genocide. *Science Advances*, 5(1), 7292.
The United Nations General Assembly. (1948). *Universal declaration of human rights* (217 [III] A). Paris.
    https://www.un.org/en/about-us/universal-declaration-of-human-rights

1. Choose the phrase that is related to each word / phrase.

1. dignity ( )
2. genocide ( )
3. fundamental ( )
4. mainstream ( )
5. intervention ( )

(a) interference
(b) mass killing of a single group
(c) normalize
(d) respect
(e) something that is very basic and important

2. Read the passage and choose the best answer to each question.

1. What is the main topic of this essay?
   (A) The differences in population growth rates by country.
   (B) The development of right-wing ideology.
   (C) The history of movements to protect human rights.
   (D) The possibility of the outbreak of World War III.

2. What did America and France do before World War II?
   (A) They made human rights laws for other countries.
   (B) They declared independence as a nation in the same year.
   (C) They made declarations on the protection of human rights.
   (D) They worked together to stop the genocide in Germany.

3. Three documents are introduced in the third paragraph. Which of them was created before 1966?
   (A) One to protect human rights worldwide.
   (B) One to protect civil and political rights.
   (C) One to protect economic, social, and cultural rights.
   (D) None of the above.

4. Which is the correct description of human rights today?
   (A) They are protected only by the constitution of each country.
   (B) No country violates human rights anymore.
   (C) Violations of human rights are internationally accepted.
   (D) They are protected by the United Nations.

5. What prompted changes in the perception of universal human rights?
   (A) States intervened in other states' affairs too much before the war.
   (B) There were excessive human rights violations during the war.
   (C) The UN put too much pressure on Germany before the war.
   (D) All nations became peaceful and equal after the war.

Writing Tips: *APA (2) In-text citations*

The referenced materials shown in the in-text citations should correspond to the documents shown in the reference list. The essay on page 52 shows three in-text citations. Match each in-text citation with the document in the reference list.

In-text citation	Reference list
(UN General Assembly, 1948)	＿＿＿ ＿＿＿＿ ＿＿＿＿ ＿＿＿＿ ＿＿＿＿ ＿＿＿＿. (1948). *Universal declaration of human rights* (217 [III] A). Paris. https://www.un.org/en/about-us/universal-declaration-of-human-rights
(＿＿＿＿, ＿＿＿＿)	Stone, L. (2019). Quantifying the Holocaust: Hyperintense kill rates during the Nazi genocide. *Science Advances*, 5(1), 7292. http://www.ebcindia.com/lawyer/articles/496_1.htm
(OHCHR, n.d.)*	＿＿＿ ＿＿＿＿ ＿＿＿＿ ＿＿＿＿ ＿＿＿＿ ＿＿＿ ＿＿＿＿ ＿＿＿＿ ＿＿＿＿. (＿.＿.). *Mainstreaming human rights.* https://www.ohchr.org/EN/newyork/Pages/MainstreamingHR.aspx

*n.d. is used when you cannot find the date of publication of the reference.

Writing Outline: *Main idea and details (2)* 2-12

Write an essay about one recent problem of law or peace. Explain in detail. Include at least two references.

Introduction	This essay will describe [problem]. I will describe what happened in detail.
Detail 1: "What"	[Problem] was....
Detail 2: "Why"	The reason why this happened is....
Detail 3: "How it ended"	[Problem] ended....
Conclusion	To summarize, [problem] happened because [why]. In the end, [how it ended].
References	

UNIT 10

Ethnicity

民族性について考えよう

How do you identify yourself?

a. Single ethnicity.

b. Mixed ethnicity.

c. A global citizen.

d. Something else.

I chose answer _____ , because .....

....

....

....

Words in Focus: *Search the internet for words and phrases.*

❏ ancestry

❏ Ariana Miyamoto

❏ Caucasian

❏ cultural background

❏ ethnicity

❏ heritage

❏ Mongolian

❏ prejudice

❏ racial identity

❏ species

PEACE　Promotion of Ethnic And Cultural Equality

What Is the Difference Between Race and Ethnicity?

There are many different ways to divide humans into groups. In 1779, a sociologist called Blumenbach suggested the following groups, known as races: Ethiopian (black), Caucasian (white), Mongolian (yellow), American (red), and Malayan (brown). However, scientists have found that skin color changes a lot over time. Also, groups of people have moved around the world. Therefore, it is not accurate to connect a skin color with a particular area.

✗ Why you should avoid the word "race."	✓ Why we recommend the word "ethnicity."
Recently, the word "race" is used less frequently. In fact, very few people on Earth belong to one "pure" ___1___. Humans have lived on Earth for more than five million years. Originally, they first appeared in Africa as one species that could stand on two legs. After that, humans moved across the globe and adapted to their surroundings. Groups of people were formed but they continued to move and mix with other groups, so even today it is hard to specifically classify people.	The word "ethnicity" is now used much more frequently than race. ___2___ is based on different factors, including location, religion, language, and ancestry. There are some countries which are thought to be almost monoethnic, including North Korea (99.9% of the population is of Korean ethnicity), Japan (98.5% Japanese), and China (91% Han Chinese). On the other hand, many countries including Singapore, South Africa, and the USA have very mixed, multi-ethnic populations.

Racial categories might be simpler to use because they rely on factors of appearance. However, this leads to mistakes which can be ___3___. Therefore, the idea of ethnicity is more accurate because it relates to several different factors. Humanity has a long and complex history. It makes sense to use a word which acknowledges this.

1. **Choose the best answer to complete the missing words in the passage.**

1. (A) age
   (B) globe
   (C) race
   (D) world

2. (A) Ethnicity
   (B) Population
   (C) Race
   (D) Skin color

3. (A) offend
   (B) offender
   (C) offending
   (D) offensive

2. Read the passage and choose the best answer to each question.

1. Which of the following arguments does the writer present first?

(A) Ideas about categorizing people rarely change.

(B) Some words used in the 18th century are not appropriate now.

(C) The word "race" should be used more often.

(D) Humanity can be divided into three races.

2. What kind of divisions are said to be appropriate today?

(A) Groups based on race.

(B) Groups based on skin color.

(C) Groups based on ethnicity.

(D) Groups based on appearance.

3. Look at the table. Which of the following sentences is true?

(A) Papua New Guinea is a low diversity country.

(B) There is only one language spoken in Tanzania.

(C) DR Congo is a more diverse country than Japan.

(D) Many languages are spoken in North Korea.

Index of ethnic (linguistic) diversity (Selected countries) Fearon (2003)		
Ranking	Country	Index
1	Papua New Guinea	1
2	Tanzania	0.953
3	DR Congo	0.933
157	Japan	0.012
158	South Korea	0.004
159	North Korea	0.002

Note.
1= the population speaks completely different languages.
0= the population all speak one language.

Fearon, J. D. (2003). Ethnic and Cultural Diversity by Country. *Journal of Economic Growth*, 8(2), 195–222.

Reading Tips: *Inference (1)*

Inference とは、文中でどのようなことが示唆されているかを推測して論じることです。前ページの文章をもとに、以下の内容が示唆されているかどうかを考えてみましょう。

What can be inferred about "race" and "ethnicity"?	Yes? No?
(a) Both "race" and "ethnicity" should be used in our daily communication.	
(b) The use of the word "ethnicity" can be discriminatory for others.	
(c) "Race" may have been used more by many people in the past.	
(d) "Ethnicity" is now a socially and politically correct term.	

2-15

Am I Japanese? The experience of mixed ethnicity kids.

The word "hafu" first appeared in Japan in the 1930s. This is a Japanese word which comes from the English word "half" and describes someone of mixed Japanese and non-Japanese ethnicity. During the 1960s and 1970s, as mixed-ethnicity singers became popular, this word became more widely used. In Japan, attitudes towards ethnicity have been based
5 on appearance, leading to complex reactions towards the backgrounds of people of mixed heritage and a lack of **empathy** from their friends.

In the 1980s, the expression "hafu-gao" became well known to describe a technique of makeup used to create an appearance combining Asian and European looks. As a result,
10 people in Japan's ideas of "Japanese" and "foreign" became strongly related to appearance. At this time, the idea of "hafu" suggested "pure" Japanese skin and eyes, mixed with foreign face shapes, noses and hair. Racial **identity** seemed to be only related to appearance, with no reference to cultural background.

15 The movie "Hafu: The Mixed Race Experience in Japan" (2013) introduced five people who had been labeled "hafu." Interest in this group of people grew even further in 2015 after Ariana Miyamoto won the prize "Miss Universe Japan." Miyamoto was born to a Japanese mother and African-American father. Growing up in Nagasaki, Japan, she faced **discrimination** from classmates who told her that they did not want to "catch" her black
20 skin color. People of mixed ethnicity in Japan are struggling with responses to their cultural heritage.

Japanese-Belgian photographer Miyazaki photographed Japanese people of mixed ethnicity. He also asked them to write some questions for others to discuss. Miyazaki's book
25 and website explore what it is like to be of mixed ethnicity in Japan. One Japanese-Canadian **respondent** explained about growing up in Japan and studying English very hard for many years. When he achieved high scores in English, he was given no praise from classmates who thought that his success was only natural due to his ethnicity. A Japanese-French **respondent** felt that, in France, she was often considered to be Japanese. When she visited Japan, she was
30 surprised that everyone considered her to be French, and she felt rejected by both cultures. Being in a minority leads to stressful misunderstandings among friends and classmates.

The word "hafu" is short and simple. On the other hand, it suggests that the person is less than a "whole." Choosing a language which avoids hurting people's feelings is one
35 way to create a more equal, less prejudiced society. For example, describe the person's dual nationalities (e.g. French-Japanese) and avoid negative nuances (e.g. mixed ethnicity). Replacing negative words with **inclusive** ones is a small change, but it has a great impact on the lives of many people.

Your Reading Speed: **454** words ÷ _____ seconds × 60 = _____ wpm

1. Choose the phrase that is related to each word / phrase.

1. empathy   (   )   **(a)** a person who answers something
2. identity   (   )   **(b)** understanding other people's feelings
3. discrimination   (   )   **(c)** broad
4. respondent   (   )   **(d)** individuality
5. inclusive   (   )   **(e)** prejudice

2. Read the passage and choose the best answer to each question.

1. What does the word "hafu" refer to?
    (A) Mixed heritage.
    (B) Singers.
    (C) Japanese ethnicity.
    (D) Lack of empathy.

2. Which concept was missing in Japan in the 1980s?
    (A) The culture of wearing makeup.
    (B) Differences between Japan and other countries.
    (C) Ethnic identity.
    (D) Reference to cultural background.

3. Which is not true about Ariana Miyamoto?
    (A) She is Japanese.
    (B) She won a contest.
    (C) All of her classmates praised her appearance.
    (D) Her parents were of different ethnicities.

4. Which of these arguments is presented in the article?
    (A) A photographer had a hard time publishing a book.
    (B) A Japanese-Canadian was highly praised for his hard work.
    (C) A woman of mixed ethnicity felt rejected both in Japan and France.
    (D) People with mixed ethnicity are likely to make many friends.

5. The writer talks about using "inclusive" words. According to the article, which is an inclusive term?
    (A) Hafu.
    (B) Foreign.
    (C) Pure.
    (D) Mixed.

A thesis statement is a statement that summarizes what the writer will discuss in his or her paper. It is usually in the last part of the introduction. Read the passage on page 58 again and fill in the underlined words to see the relationship between the thesis statement and the topic of each paragraph that follows.

1	In Japan, attitudes towards ethnicity have been based on _____ , leading to _____ _____ _____ _____ _____ _____ _____ _____ _____ _____ and _____ _____ _____ _____ _____ _____ _____ .
2	Racial identity seemed to be _____ _____ _____ _____ , with no reference to cultural background.
3	People of mixed ethnicity in Japan are _____ _____ _____ _____ _____ _____ _____ .
4	Being in a minority leads to _____ _____ _____ _____ _____ _____ _____ .

Write an essay about one type of ethnicity (not your own). Find some credible information about this ethnicity online. What can you infer about it?

Introduction	I was interested in learning more about [ethnicity] because.... Here's what I found.
Online sources	According to [Author (year)],.... In addition, [Author (year)] states that....
Inference 1	What I understood from this is....
Inference 2	I was also able to infer that....
Conclusion	[Ethnicity] seem(s) [inference 1] and [inference 2]. Therefore,....
References	

Science and Scientists

科学について考えよう

Warm-up: *Share your ideas.*

Which of the following areas of science are you most interested in?

a. Psychology and/or sociology.

b. Anthropology and/or archaeology.

c. Biology and/or chemistry.

d. Physics and/or Earth science.

I chose answer _____ , because .....
....
....
....

Words in Focus: *Search the internet for words and phrases.* 2-17

❏ experiment

❏ generalize

❏ hypothesis

❏ mystery

❏ the Nile River

❏ pseudoscience

❏ pyramid

❏ sanctuary

❏ skeptical

❏ solar clock

Feature article: The Egyptian Pyramids

Probably all of you know the Pyramids of Giza in Egypt. Yes, those three structures standing side by side along the Nile River. In fact, over 140 pyramids have been found in Egypt. But do you know what they were used for? Different scientists give different explanations. Which one do you believe?

1. Tombs

The pyramids were tombs for the Egyptian kings and their families. They were built on the west side of the Nile. This is because the direction in which the sun ☐ **1** ☐ was believed to be the place for the dead spirits. The pyramids were the sanctuaries for sending the souls of important people to heaven. The kings' mummies and burial goods have been found in some of the pyramids.

2. Solar Clock

The pyramids were made as a solar clock for measuring the cycle of the seasons. By looking at the shadows of the pyramids, the farmers were able to know when to plant and harvest their crops. The three little pyramids next to the great pyramid of Khufu were built to indicate the exact dates of the four ☐ **2** ☐.

3. Food Warehouses

The pyramids were used as grain storage warehouses. According to the Old Testament, Joseph built them to help Egyptians to ☐ **3** ☐ the drought. When the surface temperatures of a pyramid were measured, it was found that some parts were hotter than other parts. This suggests that there may be secret rooms and passages in the pyramid that have not been discovered yet.

> Which one is your favorite hypothesis? Do you have any other ideas to explain the usage of the pyramids? Do not leave the question unanswered. Do not expect scientists to tell you the answer. Try to solve the mystery yourself. That is the first step to make you a scientist.

1. **Choose the best answer to complete the missing words in the passage.**

1. (A) burns
   (B) rises
   (C) sets
   (D) shines

2. (A) crops
   (B) farmers
   (C) pyramids
   (D) seasons

3. (A) survival
   (B) survive
   (C) surviving
   (D) survivor

2. Read the passage and choose the best answer to each question.

1. What is the main topic of the article?

   (A) A way to access scientific topics.

   (B) The length of the Nile River.

   (C) The purpose of the Pyramids of Giza.

   (D) The number of pyramids in Egypt.

Pyramids of Giza

✓ See where ancient kings were buried!
✓ See where they kept their supplies!
✓ Explore ancient history!

www.pyramids.net.com

2. Look at the pamphlet. Which of the hypotheses does its writer seem to believe?

   (A) Tombs and solar clock.

   (B) Solar clock and food warehouses.

   (C) Food warehouses and tombs.

   (D) None of the above.

3. What is the first step to become a scientist according to the article?

   (A) Expect scientists to provide answers.

   (B) Ask other people for their favorite hypothesis.

   (C) Leave questions unanswered.

   (D) Try to solve mysteries with your own ideas.

Reading Tips: *Inference (2)*

Inference には、本文の内容を自分なりに咀嚼して考えるリーディング技術が必要とされます。以下の文は、前ページの **1. Tombs**、**2. Solar Clock**、**3. Food Warehouses** のどれを示唆する内容となっているのか考えてみましょう。

What can be inferred about the use of pyramids?	Usage
The pyramids may have had a practical usage for people in agriculture to know when to work.	
Ancient people may have used pyramids' rooms for other purposes than tombs.	
The pyramids may have been primarily built for burying royal families.	

Ken's diary

Dear Diary,   Friday, December 16

Today, I had an amazing discussion about pseudoscience with Sara, my friend from Egypt. Pseudoscience refers to **misleading** beliefs, theories, or practices based on false or
5 pretend facts. It started when Sara gave me a key ring as a souvenir. There was a mysterious one-eyed symbol carved into the key ring. She told me the sign would protect me from the evil eye. This is a belief that if someone looks at you with jealousy, it can cause you bad luck. Sara was convinced that it was real, but I found it hard to believe that a simple look could cause such damage.
10

Then, she pointed out the blood type test used in Japan to determine a person's personality. She seemed **skeptical**, and I agreed with her. It's not fair to judge someone's personality based on their blood type. There is no scientific evidence to support the theory. Whether it's the evil eye or blood type test, it's questionable as a science, but it doesn't harm
15 people, and it's fun to talk about.

Later in the day, we went to a cosmetics store where the salesperson was pushing a new product claiming to have magical powers to heal dry skin. The sales pitch sounded convincing. She showed us two photos of dry, dirty skin and baby-soft skin, but we were doubtful.
20 Are these photos sufficient to prove the **effectiveness** of this product? Maybe the seller was only emphasizing the results that would convince us to buy the product. Pseudoscience is problematic when it is exploited commercially.

After I came home, I read an article about researchers who fall into the trap of
25 pseudoscience. As a college student myself, I know how tempting it is to cite research results even though they are dubious. When I'm under pressure for a research paper deadline, I hear the devil telling me it's okay to cheat a little. However, it's important to base our work on solid facts. I should step back and think about the **consequences** of writing a false paper.

30 Overall, our discussion made me realize how easy it is to fall into the trap of pseudoscience. Sometimes it's fun to play with pseudoscience at a level that doesn't hurt anyone. However, there is no end to the commercialized pseudoscience exploited to profit from it. Moreover, our own research can become pseudoscience when we escape from facing the truth. I'll keep the key ring Sara gave me today to remember always to be honest with the
35 truth, and myself. This was not the original use of this symbol. Still, I think it's scientific to generalize findings and **experiment** to see if they can be applied to other fields.

Good night!
Ken

Your Reading Speed: **456** words ÷ _____ seconds × 60 = _____ wpm

1. Choose the phrase that is related to each word / phrase.

1. misleading   (   )

2. skeptical   (   )

3. effectiveness   (   )

4. consequence   (   )

5. experiment   (   )

(a) giving the wrong idea or impression

(b) the result or outcome of an action

(c) how well something works or achieves its purpose

(d) having doubts or questioning the truth

(e) to try or test new ideas

2. Read the passage and choose the best answer to each question.

1. What was the main point of today's discussion between Ken and Sara?

(A) Misleading beliefs based on pretend facts.

(B) Scientific theories originating in Egypt.

(C) Effective use of key chains.

(D) Negative emotional expressions.

2. What did both Ken and Sara think about the blood type test?

(A) It's an unscientific theory.

(B) Its results are accurate.

(C) It's supported by evidence.

(D) It can be harmful to people.

3. What did the salesperson claim about the new cosmetic product?

(A) There are many complaints about this product.

(B) It can heal dry skin magically.

(C) It is backed by good photographers.

(D) It is easy to cheat customers.

4. What is Ken's view on taking shortcuts in research?

(A) It is necessary to trap people.

(B) It has nothing to do with college students.

(C) It is acceptable to cheat a little.

(D) It will lead to severe consequences.

5. What will Ken do with the key ring Sara gave him?

(A) Keep an eye on it so Sara does not steal it.

(B) Use it to protect himself from the evil eye.

(C) Give it to someone who has a skin problem.

(D) Keep it as a reminder to be honest with himself.

In self-reflective writing, a writer reflects on past events, experiences, opinions, and so on. It is very personal, and includes formats such as diaries. Using the chart below, summarize how the diary on page 64 is structured.

Introduction (Explain important characters/setting)	Today, I had an _____ _____ _____ _____ with Sara, my friend from _____.
Beginning	Then, she pointed out the _____ _____ _____ used in Japan to _____ _____ _____ _____.
Middle	_____ _____ _____ _____, we went to a cosmetics store where the salesperson was pushing a new product claiming to have _____ _____ _____ _____ _____ _____.
End	_____ _____ _____ _____, I read an article about researchers who _____ _____ _____ _____ of pseudoscience.
Conclusion	Overall, _____ _____ _____ _____ _____ how easy it is to fall into the trap of pseudoscience.

Write about a kind of science that strongly impacts your life. What information is available? Can you trust the information? What can you infer from it? What does this mean to you?

Introduction	[Science] is a science that impacts me because.... I would like to reflect on some information I found about it online.
Online information	According to [Author (year)],....
Inference	What I understood from this is....
Self-reflection	Personally, I feel that....
Conclusion	To sum up, [science] is said to be [online information]. In my view, [self-reflection].
References	

Styles of Writing

書きことばの形式について考えよう

Warm-up: *Share your ideas.*

Which genre(s) of writing are you familiar with?

a. Expository writing.

b. Descriptive writing.

c. Persuasive writing.

d. Narrative writing.

I chose answer _____ , because . . . . .

Words in Focus: *Search the internet for words and phrases.* 2-21

❏ biography

❏ budget

❏ complimentary

❏ destination

❏ editorial

❏ expository writing

❏ genre

❏ manual

❏ poetry

❏ recommendation

2-22

Rob's Travel Blog: Where should I stay in City A?

As I've said in recent posts, in City A, it's really important to stay near City Mall, because that's where most of the action is. I don't think you want to take a long trip back to your ⬚ 1 ⬚ with loads of shopping bags! So, I would recommend Milton Hotel. It's only a 2-minute walk from City Mall. The path to the hotel is really straightforward, so you don't need to worry about losing your way.

I stayed at the Milton Hotel back in October, and it was an ⬚ 2 ⬚ experience. The staff were really nice, and helped me when I wanted to find a sandwich store. It's a business hotel, which means you can easily get Wi-Fi access. Plus, the shower and bathtub were HUGE, so it was nice to get my rest there after all of my shopping. Best of all, breakfast is free! No worries about big breakfasts eating away at your travel budget.

Rob's Happy Travel

Dear Dr. Smith,

I hope you are enjoying the nice weather.

Regarding your letter about the best places to stay in City A, my recommendation is to stay at Milton Hotel. Since you have a business meeting in City Mall, I believe this is the best option; it is only a two-minute walk from your hotel to your destination.

From my recent stay at Milton Hotel, the staff were of great assistance to me, and they offer free Wi-Fi, which I understand is very important to you. The shower and bathtub were ⬚ 3 ⬚ large. Their breakfast is complimentary.

If you are interested in more details, please go to www.MiltonHotel.co.uk. There should be more information about available rooms.

Best,
Rob Adams
Tour Director, Rob's Happy Travel

---

1. **Choose the best answer to complete the missing words in the passage.**

1. (A) country
   (B) hotel
   (C) house
   (D) store

2. (A) awesome
   (B) awkward
   (C) impractical
   (D) inconvenient

3. (A) suffice
   (B) a sufficient
   (C) sufficiently
   (D) insufficient

2. Read the passage and choose the best answer to each question.

1. Which of the following does the blog NOT mention about Milton Hotel?

   (A) It is located close to a lively part of the town.

   (B) Shopping bags can be delivered to guest rooms.

   (C) Easy internet access is offered.

   (D) Guests will be able to relax in a large bathroom.

2. Which best describes the writer of the letter?

   (A) A doctor.　　　(B) A tourist.　　(C) A travel agent.　　(D) A friend.

3. Look at the chart. Which hotel is also likely to be suitable for Dr. Smith?

   (A) Eastern Hotel.　　(B) Hitz Plaza.　　(C) Best Resort.　　(D) None of them.

	Eastern Hotel	Hitz Plaza	Best Resort
Location	10 minutes from City Mall	Within City Mall	30 minutes from City Mall
Breakfast	Complimentary	Complimentary	Not provided
Business facilities	Wi-Fi ($10/night)	Free Wi-Fi	N/A
Bathroom	Spacious	Spacious	Shower only

Reading Tips: *Paraphrasing*

文の内容を自分の言葉で言い換えたりまとめたりする手法は、paraphrasing と呼ばれます。この手法は、他人の文献をそのままコピーして書く剽窃行為 (plagiarism) を防ぎつつ、情報を自分のライティングに取り入れるためにも有効です。前ページのブログと手紙の内容を言い換えたものです。下線部の単語を本文から書き出しましょう。

Travel agent and blogger _____ _____ recommends _____ _____ as a place to stay when visiting _____ _____. The main reason he recommends this hotel is its proximity to the _____ _____, which is _____ _____-_____ _____ away. He also lists other attractive points of _____ _____, such as the friendliness of the _____, the easy _____ access, the comfort of the _____, and the _____ _____ service.

Genres of writing: How are they different?

There are many different ways of writing. Sometimes you might write to tell a story, or write in order to help someone use a smartphone application. You might even email a message to your parents to convince them to buy you a new computer. Here, you will be introduced to the four main **genres** of writing in English: expository, descriptive, persuasive, and narrative.
5 While you are reading, think about what kinds of writing you might have seen before, or have tried writing already!

First, what is expository writing? It relates facts. Newspapers, textbooks, and instruction manuals are good examples of expository writing. It does not include types of
10 newspaper articles such as editorials and opinion pieces. What is most important about this type of writing is that it does not include the author's personal opinion. For example, you usually do not see a sentence such as "Setting up this smartphone is a **pain in the neck**," within a smartphone manual.

15 Next, let us move onto descriptive writing. This type of writing aims to "help the reader visualize, **in detail**, a character, event, place, or all of these things at once" (Traffis, 2020). In good descriptive writing, the author describes things in terms of the five senses, which are smell, touch, taste, sound, and sight. You might see this type of writing in personal diaries and poetry.
20

Now, what about persuasive writing? It shows the author's opinion, and also tries to convince the reader that this opinion is valid (Traffis, 2020). For example, you might have already written essays to defend your view about **controversial** topics. You can also use persuasive writing in job applications. In this case, you try to convey to the employer why you
25 are a good candidate for the job.

Finally, let us end with narrative writing. Narrative writing basically tells a story, where a series of events occurs in some chronological order. Therefore, all types of fiction and biographies fit into this **genre** of writing. Narrative writing is different from descriptive
30 writing, because it contains lots of action. The author also tends to use a **first-person** point of view, using "I" or "my." On the other hand, descriptive writing does not need action, since it just paints a picture of a character, event, or place.

This essay presented a description of four different **genres** of writing: expository,
35 descriptive, persuasive, and narrative. While you study English, think about which **genre** your writing or reading assignment falls into. In this way, you can begin to understand why certain things are written the way they are, or what the author wants to achieve with their writing. Moreover, you may start to find that many good written pieces are actually a combination of these different **genres** of writing.

> Your Reading Speed: **465** words ÷ _____ seconds × 60 = _____ wpm

Reference
Traffis, C. (2020). *Learn the types of writing: Expository, descriptive, persuasive, and narrative.* Grammarly Blog.
    https://www.grammarly.com/blog/types-of-writing/

1. Choose the phrase that is related to each word / phrase.

1. genre   (   )   **(a)** a type of text
2. pain in the neck   (   )   **(b)** annoying
3. in detail   (   )   **(c)** causing disagreement or dispute
4. controversial   (   )   **(d)** referring directly to the writer
5. first-person   (   )   **(e)** thoroughly

2. Read the passage and choose the best answer to each question.

1. According to the author, what counts as a type of "writing"?
   (A) Instructions for a smartphone app.
   (B) An email to your parents.
   (C) A story about your summer vacation.
   (D) All of the above.

2. Which of the following is NOT an example of expository writing?
   (A) A scientific report.
   (B) An essay about recent news.
   (C) A magazine article about pets.
   (D) A story about magical creatures.

3. The word "visualize" in descriptive writing is closest in meaning to…
   (A) Improve eyesight.
   (B) Imagine.
   (C) Daydream.
   (D) Fiction.

4. Which is the best example of persuasive writing?
   (A) This essay, "Genres of Writing: How are they different?"
   (B) A report about a sports game in a magazine.
   (C) An online advertisement for a new book.
   (D) An essay on the pros and cons of school uniforms.

5. What does the author conclude?
   (A) Writers should restrict their writing to one genre.
   (B) It is useful to consider what the genre should be when writing.
   (C) Genre is more important for reading than writing assignments.
   (D) Some genres of writing are better than others.

When you cite a reference in-text, it can be either (1) a direct quote (you use a phrase that is straight from the reference) or (2) a paraphrase (you put the information in your own words). From the passage on page 70, find examples and fill in the chart below.

Type of in-text citation	"Genres of Writing: How are they different?"
(1) Direct Quote	"help the reader _____, _____ _____, _____ _____, _____, _____, _____ _____ _____ _____ _____ _____ _____" (Traffis, 2020).
(2) Paraphrase	It shows the author's _____, and also tries to _____ _____ _____ _____ _____ _____ _____ _____ (Traffis, 2020).

 2-24

Find two pieces of advice online for students of English as a Foreign Language. What do they suggest? Paraphrase one, and quote directly from the other.

Introduction	There is a lot of advice provided for learners of English as a Foreign Language. I found advice about [source 1] and [source 2].
Source 1	According to [Author (year)],...
Source 2	[Author (year)] recommends "_____."
Summary	To sum up, learners of English should [source 1] and [source 2]. In my opinion,....
References	

参考文献

Unit 1

Bennett, K. (2009). English academic style manuals: A survey. *Journal of English for Academic Purposes*, *8*(1), 43–54.

Unit 2

Asada, K., Mitsutake, R., Hashimoto, S., & Sagimori, H. (2020, September 23). *Impending crisis of aging doctors treating aging patients*. Nikkei Asia.

International Labour Organization. (2020, July 16). *Practical guide on teleworking during the COVID-19 pandemic and beyond*.

Moor, L. (2021, November 9). Furusato nozei: An introduction to Japan's hometown tax program. *Tokyo Weekender*. https://www.tokyoweekender.com/japan-life/furusato-nozei-japan-hometown-tax/

Unit 4

World Economic Forum. (2020). *Global gender gap report*. https://www.weforum.org/reports/gender-gap-2020-report-100-years-pay-equality/

Unit 5

Deshmukh, A. (2022, February 11). *Mapped: The world's major religions*. https://www.visualcapitalist.com/mapped-major-religions-of-the-world/

Unit 8

Morishita, S. (2021). What is omotenashi? A comparative analysis with service and hospitality in the Japanese lodging industry. *Journal of Advanced Management Science*, *9*(4), 88–95.

Unit 9

The Office of the High Commissioner for Human Rights. (n.d.). *Mainstreaming human rights*. https://www.ohchr.org/EN/newyork/Pages/MainstreamingHR.aspx

Stone, L. (2019). Quantifying the Holocaust: Hyperintense kill rates during the Nazi genocide. *Science Advances*, *5*(1), 7292.

The United Nations General Assembly. (1948). *Universal declaration of human rights*. https://www.un.org/en/about-us/universal-declaration-of-human-rights

Unit 10

Fearon, J. D. (2003). Ethnic and cultural diversity by country. *Journal of Economic Growth, 8*(2), 195–222.

Nagata, M. (2015, Aug 6). Not Japanese enough? Miss Universe Japan looks to fight prejudice. *Nichi Bei*. https://metropolisjapan.com/the-world-of-ariana-miyamoto/

Miyazaki, T. (n.d.) *Hāfu2Hāfu*. https://hafu2hafu.org/

Nishikura, M., & Perez Takagi, L. (Producer/Directors). (2013). *Hafu* [Motion picture]. Japan: Distribber.

Unit 12

Traffis, C. (2020). Learn the types of writing: Expository, descriptive, persuasive, and narrative. *Grammarly Blog*. https://www.grammarly.com/blog/types-of-writing/

TEXT PRODUCTION STAFF

| edited by | 編集 |
| Hiroko Nakazawa | 中澤 ひろ子 |

| English-language editing by | 英文校正 |
| Bill Benfield | ビル・ベンフィールド |

| cover design by | 表紙デザイン |
| Nobuyoshi Fujino | 藤野 伸芳 |

| text design by | 本文デザイン |
| Nobuyoshi Fujino | 藤野 伸芳 |

CD PRODUCTION STAFF

narrated by	吹き込み者
Dominic Allen (American English)	ドミニク・アレン（アメリカ英語）
Jack Merluzzi (American English)	ジャック・マルジ（アメリカ英語）
Jennifer Okano (American English)	ジェニファー・オカノ（アメリカ英語）
Karen Hedrick (American English)	カレン・ヘドリック（アメリカ英語）

Global Perspectives
Reading & Writing Book 2

2024年1月10日　初版印刷
2024年1月20日　初版発行

編著者　中西 のりこ　Nicholas Musty　大竹 翔子

　　　　Tam Shuet Ying　Mary Ellis

発行者　佐野 英一郎

発行所　株式会社 成 美 堂
　　　　〒101-0052 東京都千代田区神田小川町 3-22
　　　　TEL 03-3291-2261　　　FAX 03-3293-5490
　　　　http://www.seibido.co.jp

印刷・製本　（株）倉敷印刷

ISBN 978-4-7919-7285-2　　　　　　　　　　　　Printed in Japan